The Holy CEO

An Autobiography

Christian Fabre

Swami Pranavananda Brahmendra Avadhuta

JAICO PUBLISHING HOUSE

Ahmedabad Bangalore Bhopal Chennai
Delhi Hyderabad Kolkata Lucknow Mumbai

Published by Jaico Publishing House
A-2 Jash Chambers, 7-A Sir Phirozshah Mehta Road
Fort, Mumbai - 400 001
jaicopub@jaicobooks.com
www.jaicobooks.com

THE HOLY CEO: AN AUTOBIOGRAPHY
ISBN 978-81-8495-198-1

First Jaico Impression: 2011

Printed by
Repro India Limited
Plot No. 50/2, T.T.C. MIDC Industrial Area
Mahape, Navi Mumbai - 400 710.

CONTENTS

INTRODUCTION

An unsuspecting young Frenchman, by the name of Christian Fabre, landed in Madras in the early '70s. A tumultuous series of paradoxical events led to his becoming a complete destitute with no job, no money, no wife, and no son, to becoming Swami Pranavananda Brahmendra Avadhuta, and after many failed ventures, the CEO of a fashion empire. Ironically, it is the very name he renounced that is becoming popular all over India today, as more Christian Fabre stores open in numerous cities.

After his ordainment as a Naga Swami (naked Hindu monk), his beloved Guru gave him an astounding directive — his career in fashion apparel had to be his *sadhana* (spiritual practice); he had to be in the marketplace, but not of it; to bring spirituality into the material world.

Successfully straddling the seemingly opposing worlds of spirituality and international business, the press calls him the 'anti-Trump' or the 'naked emperor of ready-to-wear'.

This kind, loving, and generous maverick has founded his company on the principles of love, honesty, and respect. From the huge profits they turn over, he pays himself only 200 Euro a month and owns nothing personally. He directly, and indirectly, employs many people. Once a month he retreats to his hermitage for a week where he is free to roam naked, and be one with Nature.

Here is his life's story, in his own words...

1

YOU'VE CERTAINLY COME A LONG WAY

Year: 2008

Wow! What a view!

Cape Town spreads down the slope of the Table Mountain to the ocean, where in the distance, soon to be covered by a blanket of low clouds, is Robben Island. That is where Nelson Mandela, like many others who dared to rebel against apartheid, spent many years of their lives. On the windy top of the mountain, our team of designers, Sai, Linto, and Ani; one of our executives Benhur (yes, that is his name); my assistant John; and I, are happily posing for pictures with this great city below us and the clouds above serving as the backdrop. Rolling down to the sea, we first see the colourful little houses, then further down are the tall buildings of the city centre, and then the harbour. To the right is the huge stadium where the Soccer World Cup 2010 took place. This spectacular view stirs my mind and takes me back to the years I spent in Madras, South India, where I lived once, starving, fighting against all odds, not knowing what to do next to survive. Never would I have dreamt that one day I would be standing here in Africa with such a talented team. I thought to myself, you certainly have come a long way...

This specific trip was brought about by a journalist and his team from Channel 4 who came to Chennai and then to our hermitage to shoot a documentary for Discovery Channel, which was later shown in more than 75 countries. It was only after it was aired that I understood that the documentary was a series about very rich famous men! This was quite ironic, because they were featuring me, a man earning not more than 200 Euros per month, clubbed together with these multi-millionaires! I was shocked. However, the documentary had drawn the attention of many people from different countries. To this day, I receive messages from around the world. Most messages are positive, some of them are from people asking for help, and very few are from people interested in the spiritual aspect of what we do. Some viewers wanted to see if they could do business with us. They didn't seem to realise from the documentary that I do not own anything and that all the profits our company makes, is distributed amongst the workers.

But, the mere prospect of our 'Christian Fabre' brand being distributed and sold in South Africa was very interesting for us, because the people who had made this proposal had showed real interest in our profit-sharing system. So, in January 2008, we decided to visit our friend Tom, his partner Nico and his charming wife Christie, to see how we could work together.

We had a marvellous reception in South Africa and also shot a programme for *Top Billing*, a popular local television show, and gave interviews to a local magazine that had the largest circulation in South Africa. We were put up in a luxurious hotel on a wine farm and our whole team relished the good food and drink. How lucky we felt to have this 'holiday cum work' opportunity.

We were taken to beautiful places around Cape Town and our team beamed with happiness on being treated like royalty. It gave us not only hope, but also the desire to be able to do good business in a country we did not know at all, which looked so promising to us.

Unfortunately, the financial turmoil, which began in July 2008, affected South Africa as well and forced us to put this dream in abeyance, awaiting a better moment. I still have not lost hope that we will succeed there as soon as the global economic picture stabilises and improves.

Nevertheless, let's go back to the very beginning of this journey to what I remember about my childhood.

2

MY SUPER SHIRTS

I was born on June 8, 1942, in Beziers, Languedoc, southern France, to great loving parents. My father was a self-made man. When he was 15, his mother had run away with another man, leaving her husband and abandoning her five children. My father had to stop studying, and start working to help support his brothers and sisters. His hunger for knowledge was such that he devoured whatever book he could lay his hands on. He would read to us passages that he particularly liked, or that had touched him. He was a cabinet-maker and made graceful Louis XV-style chairs, but out of economic necessity at the time, he was employed with the French National Railways (SNCF). We never had any sophisticated toys, but he made fantastic ones with wood. I still remember a beautiful airplane with propellers. I was much envied by my friends for that. I was and still am very proud of my father.

My mother was of Spanish origin. Her parents had run away from the Civil War and landed in Beziers, where she met my father, a French man of pure Languedoc roots. They raised their four children with very little money, but the family spirit, which is a rare thing in France today, nurtured us. I was to find this again in India one day. We were a tightly knit family and always lent a helping hand to each other.

When I was two years old, the SNCF transferred my father to Cerbere, a small picturesque village of about 1000 people, in French Catalona, in the Eastern Pyrenees, just before you cross the border into Spain. Our house clung to the mountain, with the *garrigue* (bush land) on one side and on the steep slopes down to the blue sea, with dark rocks and secluded beaches that tourists had not invaded and spoilt.

School was at the bottom of the mountain, next to the beach where fishermen had their boats waiting for the next launch. I remember that when I was around four years old, my school friends and I would piss standing on top of the railway bridge onto the cars below. The drivers would think it was raining and would switch on their windscreen wipers.

At this young age, I used to skip classes often, because I preferred frolicking in the waves between the rocks and catching small squids, or picking up mussels, or sea urchins, with my bare hands. Alternatively, I used to follow the goats up the mountain. One day, I noticed a healthy goat down a ravine and I wanted to chase it away by throwing a stone at it. I bent to pick up the stone, found it too heavy for me, and ultimately went, with the stone, rolling down the ravine.

Fortunately, there was sand at the bottom and I only had a broken arm and a bleeding head from a few scratches. A goatkeeper climbed down, picked me up, and brought me back to my mother who screamed in fright on seeing my head covered in blood.

That wasn't the only time I scared my mother. Once, I got lost in the mountains and the whole village was called to help and find me. My parents did not punish me, because they were only too happy to see me alive. The only time I was slapped was when I told my father, 'But you are dumb...' I had just read that word and had not understood what it meant. Boom! My father's hand struck me heavily. My cheek still burns. 'That will teach you to find the real meaning of your words before you use them. Turn your tongue seven times in your mouth before you utter a new word.'

In winter, when the Tramotane (local regular wind in this part of Languedoc) blew strongly, it was cold indeed. 'Too cold to throw a cat outside,' as we say in our area. For dinner, we gathered close together in front of the fireplace where the dead wood that my father had collected in the mountain was our only source of heat. Our body would feel burning hot in front and freezing cold at the back.

We did not have much to eat during the last World War, but my parents fed us by growing our own vegetables in a small garden we tended to on the land that belonged to the SNCF. My mother made an excellent brew from the seeds of wild plants that she collected from the nearby hills and we called it 'coffee'. She loved the chickens that she raised at the back of the house. She was very kind to them and took great care of them, so much so that we were never short of eggs. I can still recall watching my mother forcefully, yet lovingly, giving a spoonful of hot wine and sugar to a sick chick.

My father knew the surrounding Pyrenees Mountains like the back of his hand and used to help freedom fighters, and people who wanted to avoid the German army patrols and escape into Spain, from where they would find their way to the UK or anywhere in the world.

Sometimes he would hide them in the coal wagon next to the steam engine to go through the tunnel that separated our village Cerbere from the Spanish village Port Bou on the other side of the mountain, which was a natural border between the two countries. One evening, German soldiers knocked on our door while we were sitting around the fireplace. We were all petrified, but the German officer smiled, and said, 'We are good German people.'

They had smelt the coffee my mother was brewing and were hoping to be offered some.

On Sundays, I worked at my uncle's pastry bakery. He made wonderfully delicious *mille-feuilles* (thousand leaves cake), the best in the whole country. People came from faraway places to queue up and buy his cakes. I was paid five old Francs (equivalent of 0.05 of the new Franc). That is about one cent of our actual Euro... almost nothing, but enough for me to watch a movie at the local cinema, it made me feel like a man.

It was during this period that I fell ill. It was called 'the disease of the Kings', as haemophilia is a genetic disease transmitted from male to male within the same family, and the Kings of Spain were known not to live beyond 40 years of age because of this disease. I used to bleed even if a fork pricked me. I had blood in my urine and if I cut myself with a knife, I could bleed like a chicken. I was not allowed to play with the other young boys because if I were to receive a blow, I could bleed internally. I had no option but to watch my friends playing rough games. It was a probability that I would not live beyond 40, but I am 67 years old now and still very much alive, thanks to my parents' relentless love and the treatment I got from our village doctor, who hailed from Madagascar. It was clearly not my Karma to die young. After about three years, the disease was completely in remission, never to trouble me again.

When I was seven, my father was transferred again and we moved back to Beziers. The war was over. After the *garrigue*, the sea, and the mountains, we felt like we were in prison. We lived in a little house dating back to the Middle Ages, in the old part of Beziers. The street was so narrow that one could see and hear what the neighbours were doing and saying.

However, the ambience was friendly. At sunset we would take the chairs out into the street where the men were discussing current subjects, the women were knitting, and the children were playing 'Jacks' with marbles in the dry gutters. My father had just bought the first TV set in the whole street and the people of the area would come home to watch American movies. I was proud.

I was sent to our local school called Lakanal. During that epoch in France, these communal schools were human and warm. I remained in that school until the age of 14, long enough for me to acquire a good amount of general knowledge that has been very helpful throughout my life.

In those days, there were not as many Maghrebians (people from Morocco, Algeria, or Tunisia) as there are now, and machines for harvesting grapes didn't exist yet, so many poor families like us in Beziers, used to work in the vineyards during the harvest season which always fell at the end of the summer holidays. It was really a welcome opportunity for my family, because it enabled us to buy schoolbooks and my mother could then afford cloth to make our clothes. Therefore, every year, from when I was eight years old until my military obligation at the age of 19, my mother, brothers, sister, and I had to go to the fields to cut grapes. In Languedoc, the grape tree is kept short and is not allowed to creep along high wires.

I did not like to harvest grapes as it was either too hot, or it was raining and we had to work with our feet squelching in the mud, and all the time the owner would shout at us to work faster and not forget a single grape on the ground, or behind hidden leaves.

Sometimes, when the vines were too low, my back ached so much that I came to hate this work and the *Meneuse* (a woman hired to work fast and set the pace) began to shout and say horrible things about our skills when we were too far behind. Later on, when I grew older and stronger, I was employed to carry the *comporte* (a big wooden container) in which the grapes were collected and transported to the horse-drawn carriage. We were paid 10 old francs per day, plus two bottles of wine... extremely hard work. Today, when I pass by those vineyards it reminds me of my mother, who when she saw me lagging behind, would come over and help me work faster and give me courage. When work on the landlord's vineyard was over, we were still not done with grape harvesting. Once the harvest was over, the landlords would allow anyone to get into the vineyard and harvest the grapes left behind. It was a practice that goes back to the Middle Ages and was called 'grappling'. Our father used to take us all to a faraway vineyard so we could harvest our own wine for the whole year. It was fun to squash the grapes with our feet. After some time, the fumes from the fermenting grapes would give us a bit of a high and we had loads of fun.

Later on, I realised that I had been through the greatest school in life and I am thankful to my father and mother for all these experiences.

My mother was a remarkable seamstress and she made everything we wore, except the shoes (if she knew how to make them, she would have). Whenever I spotted a nice fashionable shirt, in a store in town, I would take my mother there so that she could see the model displayed in the window. She would then ask me, 'Do you like that one?' And while standing there she would carefully note down all the small details, because she did not dare enter the store. Back home, she would immediately make the pattern before she forgot the design. Together then, we would go to a fabric shop and select my choice. She would replicate the design, and sometimes it would be better than the original.

My friends admired my new shirts. 'Wow! where did you buy it? It is a super shirt,' they would say. All her life, she continued to make our clothes, shirts, trousers, coats, jackets, gloves, mufflers, and caps.

My grandmother ran a garment store. My mother helped her in the shop and as a seamstress she made fashionable clothes for the customers. She must have passed those genes to me.

In those days, my mother hesitated to send me to learn Catechism, since my father, a member of the communist party, did not want to hear about it. I liked it though, and used to get mystical feelings. After my first communion, knowing my father to be a staunch unbeliever, the priest offered to come and persuade my father that I should become a Catholic priest. Despite the oral prowess of the priest, my father stubbornly told him, 'As long as I am alive, there will be no priest in the family!' All my devout feelings did not however prevent me from having fun and a good time during the late '50s and early '60s in Beziers.

We organised huge parties then. It was the era of Elvis Presley. My dad had given me a record player as a gift. I loved rock 'n roll and was a rather good dancer. This was a helpful skill, what with all the girls around me. My first girlfriend was gorgeous, but I soon forgot her name. We used to sing songs by Paul Anka together. I told her, 'You have beautiful eyes.' In fact, what were more beautiful than her eyes were her boobs!

After Lakanal School, I attended the local Lycée Henri-IV where I received a Baccalaureate with Literature as the main subject, followed by a period in a private school of Commerce. I did not have any further physical or metaphysical problems. During the weekends, we took our record player, collected a few bottles of good wine, gathered the girls, and went to my friend Stephane's chateau, which had plenty of bedrooms to go around.

We had great fun, and it was all clean… no drugs, no hard alcohol. After all, it was summer, in the south of France, when Swedish girls would come down to the seaside, 13 km from our town. We would hitchhike to Valras-Plage, or to Capd'Age, where the beaches were long, clean, and deserted. There were pink flamingos all over the lagoon as far as the eyes could see. We were naked on the beach with the Swedish girls. I never had to make an effort for the girls to like me.

Then came the time for the military service.

3

NIGHT OF THE JACKAL

I found myself in the Montelimar Barracks learning how to read and type Morse code, use a gun and hike in the wilderness under a hot sun, carrying a shoulder bag filled with a very heavy radiotelephone. I did not like being in the army, or their stubborn discipline. 'I don't want to know!' the sergeant would scream at us.

My new life came as a shock to me. Denied freedom, I used to jump over the barrack's wall to go for a movie with friends, or to see the girls. When I was caught, they sent me to the 'hole'. They removed my belt and shoelaces and I would find myself alone in the barrack's prison cell. I think this is perhaps where I started to meditate.

Since then, I remain a staunch anti-militarist and abide by Mahatma Gandhi's principle of *Ahimsa* (non-violence).

In 1961, right in the middle of the Algerian War, I found myself in Tizi-Ouzou. At first it was rather fun, we used to go out with the guys from the Foreign Legion who would call out to us, 'Hey guys, how about having a frothy one (beer) with us?' They could even remove bottle caps with their teeth! As far as I was concerned, it was evident that the people of Algeria should be independent and I was wondering what the hell I was doing there. Protecting the interests of rich French colonialists? My elder brother participated as a soldier in this war in Algeria before me and so did my younger brother. Imagine my mother's worries and anguish.

We had to defend our helicopter base. 'Fellagas' entered at night and did horrible things to us French soldiers. They used to disappear from the base as swiftly as they came in. I had never killed a man, but one night as I was on guard duty along the electric fence of barbed wires, I saw a pair of eyes shining in the darkness.

'Who is there?' I called out thrice.

I had no other choice, I fired at those bright eyes, heard a 'couic', and thought I had killed a man. The whole base woke up. They switched on the big floodlights and sent out patrols. I had killed a jackal. Everyone had a good laugh at my expense. For me, though, it was important that I had not killed a human being.

There was also the military brothel with French whores, because guys were telling us horror stories about soldiers who had sex with Arab women. They scared us with tales about razor blades in the women's vaginas and emasculated men running out screaming, holding their groin.

We queued outside the brothel's door and the officer would scream:

'Next!'

While one man would come out buttoning up his pants, the other one, red-faced, entered the room.

'Next!'

It was my turn. All the tales had conjured up nightmares in my mind... I could not enter the room... I was suddenly afraid, afraid I would die.

Kabylie was a beautiful country and the 'Kabils' a very refined people — proud, white-skinned and some of them had piercing blue eyes. I loved warm climates and started to learn Arabic. At one point in time, I decided to stay in Algeria because I was offered a job there once the war was over, but my father did not agree. I was released from my military obligations in June 1963 and went back to Beziers as a Sergeant.

4

A NEW PAGE

Since I still felt a little unsettled after my time in the army, my father suggested that I take some time off to find my bearings again. He left me to enjoy a holiday on the beach at the Cap.

Not too long after that, my father told me, 'It is now time that you work and earn a living.'

Therefore, on the first of September, I became a ticket collector at the exit of the Gagny-East Station (in the suburbs of Paris). It was hard for a guy like me, who had spent all his life until then in a sunny, warm country. I earned 650 old Francs (about 95 Euros) per month and the dormitory of the SNCF (French National Railways) cost me 350. I was left with 300 old Francs to feed myself, so by the fifteenth of each month I had nothing left except enough to buy myself a piece of bread and some sugar with which I had to make do for breakfast and lunch. I was sleeping through dinner. For six months, I did not make a single friend and I was getting more and more depressed.

There were strikes all the time, and people behaved in a sinister way. I had to sweep the station platforms as well, and I was freezing. I got desperate for another job. Working for the SNCF was definitely not for me.

Just before my military service, my father had sent me to England for six months, an exchange between sons and daughters of the national railways. I spoke reasonably good English as I had lots of practice with the British girls of Stoke-On-Trent. Bluffing my way in, I got a job as an interpreter in a travel agency on Avenue d'Iena in Paris. They asked me to take a language test and I was accepted. I had to go to Orly airport to pick up rich American tourists, bring them safely to their hotel, and then show them Paris by night.

I did this job for nearly six years. We were paid on a commission basis. There were months when I earned well and other times, especially during the lean tourist periods, when it was difficult. The great advantage was that as a travel agent employee, I could travel by air on reduced fares and was offered great discounts on hotel prices all over the world. In the first year, I managed to travel on my own to New York, Miami, and Puerto Rico. Wow! What a great feeling to walk down Fifth Avenue, my nose up in the sky, feeling totally amazed by all the skyscrapers, swimming on Miami Beach, walking down Collins Avenue... what a change from the not-so-far-behind days, when I was freezing my butt off, cleaning the railway station at Gagny-East in France.

Working in Paris was great as it allowed me to make many friends and I used to go out every night. In 1964, I was asked to interview a young woman for the post of secretary in our travel agency. She was a Franco-Japanese girl and very pretty. Two years later, we were married and soon after that, our son Nicolas was born.

My job commissions were not enough to feed three people and I found a job in a real estate agency called Cori, a division of Paribas Bank. It was a good finance school for me and I learnt a lot about banking systems, sales psychology, and accounting. Probably like it is for most newlywed couples, life was not always easy. We lived in the suburbs of Paris, in a place called 'Kremlin-Bicetre'. It was bang on an intersection on one side and a cemetery on the other side. It was an ugly place. Our baby would scream most nights and my wife who came from a well-to-do family had problems adapting herself to this change in status. Maybe we got married too quickly. I remembered my mother telling me, 'Why do you want to get married now? You are only 24!' I should have listened to her, but love is blind, I guess.

I longed to go back to the Midi (south of France), to be in the sun again. I fondly recalled the Southern French accent and the bonhomie of the people in the south. Fortunately, my employer gave me an offer to take care of the sales of some of his projects in my native place. I grabbed the opportunity and we found ourselves in Argeles, on the Mediterranean coast, a stone's throw from Spain. I had to sell holiday houses built on the rocky seaside in Banyuls, near Cerbere. Strangely, with Cori-Paribas Bank, the more we sold, the less we got paid…

One of my customers, who headed Kreglinger France, a trading company in wool and leather, was impressed by my selling capabilities and suggested that I divert my attentions to the leather business and work for them.

'But I don't know anything about wool or leather!'

'Well, then you shall learn,' he shot back at me.

I resigned and left for a training course in Mezamet, the then leather centre in France. In the beginning, there was talk of me going to New Zealand, but as the world wool price had crashed, I was offered a post in Madras. 'Where is Madras?' I asked. I had never heard of a town named Madras. As far as I knew it was the name of a colourfully checkered fabric. 'In India', I was told and I was posted there as a buyer of semi-tanned leather. A page in the book of my life had been turned.

5

SHOCKING INDIA

On October 26, 1971, I landed in Bombay with wife, child, and luggage in tow. Stepping out of the plane, our first impression of India was the shock of the temperature — a humid, asphyxiating heat, sticking to our skins. The airport was dirty. While waiting in an endless queue, my little son Nicolas started to vomit. This adventure had not started very well.

At Madras airport, Andre, the guy whom I was replacing from my company, was waiting for us. He dropped us for the night at the Woodlands Hotel, the best one in the city in those days. The three of us had to share a bed with stained bedsheets, mosquitoes, and a cockroach that roamed around the bathroom. We were close to turning around and returning to our home country at once. The next day, things looked a little less sinister. Andre took us to his residence that was soon to become ours. In the afternoon, we went to the Muslim areas of the city that specialised in the leather business and he introduced me to various tanners and leather dealers. I could not understand a word of the English they were speaking. There was the suffocating heat again and I was wondering what the hell I was doing there. At 5 pm, he asked me to drop him at the airport in our company car, a Fiat 140, which left thick black smoke in our wake. The car was using more oil than petrol!

At the airport, a boy was waiting for us with Andre's luggage. Andre gave me the car keys and those of the apartment. He wished me good luck, we shook hands, and turning around, he quickly disappeared inside the airport building. This guy had only one thing in mind — to leave Madras as soon as possible. I stood alone in the departure lounge for a while.

Driving on the left side of the road now, in a city I did not know, it took me three hours to find the house again, which became our first home in India, only to discover my wife standing on a chair, terrified and screaming, because of her first encounter with a gecko (lizard). I had to chase away all visible reptiles before she would go to sleep. After falling asleep with much difficulty, we were awakened in the middle of the night by strange noises. It seemed as if someone was trying to get into the house. But, it was the *chowkidar* (watchman) hitting his *lathi* (stick) on the ground to reassure us, and the landlady residing below, that he was not asleep. Thanks for sharing, friend!

It was not at all easy to work in India in the '70s. My main duties were to source, negotiate the right prices, and monitor quality control of the required skins of semi-finished vegetable tanned leather, destined to be shipped to my superiors at Kreglinger. I had to go to the Muslim areas of Madras since, traditionally, they dealt in leather tanning and related businesses.

Hindus consider cows sacred and will neither kill the animal, nor do business using its by-products. It was suffocatingly hot in the factories, not to even mention the horrible stench of the tanning process.

During the quality control process, performed prior to shipping the skins abroad, I was often astonished to see many defective skins that looked exactly like the ones I had already seen and discarded as unfit for export. Understanding the trick after a while, I decided to use my fingernail to mark a cross on the rejected skins so that I could identify them without doubt and without argument. Communicating with people in other countries was not easy either. Letters took 15 days to reach France, and we had no access to fax machines or computers. We had a telex machine, but it was very difficult to get a line. To make an international phone call was quite a task, as we had to book our call about two hours ahead of time. The operator would then call us back to inform us that the number we wanted was either busy or not responding and then we had to book again. Another two hours' wait! Apart from the British Club, entertainment was scarce and the newspapers, magazines, or radio were not in French. Television had not yet reached Madras in those days and would not have been in French anyway as this was before the days of the satellite dish.

On the rare occasion that I would see newspapers or magazines in French, it would usually be three to four weeks old...tough for a Frenchman.

As my wife, son, and I were settling into our new home far away from home, we got acquainted with the household staff, inherited from my predecessor, along with the apartment that also served as my office. The beaming dark-skinned team was made up of a cook and a servant-cleaner-cum-caretaker-cum-office boy. They were the first Indians we were constantly interacting with, from the very first day. In a strange country with the combination of constant high humidity and heat comparable to a steam bath, these two Indian men were our only local contact apart from my business connections in town. They were the first faces we saw when we woke up in the morning and the last ones we saw before retiring to our bedroom for the night.

It was important for my wife and me that our lifestyle did not shock these people whose culture we did not know, so we tried our best to be civil around them. But we noticed that they would come into our bedroom and even bathrooms unannounced and it did not seem to be much of a problem to them. Whether we were in each other's arms, or undressed, did not seem to bother them one bit. Was it their curiousity bringing them in or genuine unconcern? I still do not know, after 37 years in this country, if an employee in our office or a servant at home, will come in whenever they feel like it.

One of these men was very helpful and genuinely nice to my wife, my son, and me. He would go out of his way to help us get whatever we needed.

I discovered that India was a country with the highest number of government holidays in the world. The important occasions observed by Hindus, Muslims, Buddhists, and Christians have to be considered by the government and almost each of the fourteen states that formed the Republic of India then, has its own New Year. I am not even mentioning the holidays people are forced to take during strikes (a national sport), when a leader died, sick leaves, etc. Modern India has also been initiated into the cult of celebrating politician's birthdays. The politician may be dead since eternity and no one will even remember their name or what they had achieved for India, during their lifetimes, but even then, each year, millions of rupees are spent and thousands of hours of work lost for the sake of depositing a wreath of flowers at the *samadhis* (mausoleums) of these illustrious unknowns.

As the months passed by, I decided to get a driver, as negotiating the Indian traffic was making me more and more nervous. Also, my wife and child had to be driven to school, shopping, and the Club while I was working in Periamet, the leather district of Madras.

One day I was at home, relaxing after a hot day in the ill-smelling tanneries, my wife and son were at the Club, she was probably playing bridge or playing tennis as many idle expatriate women members did, and my son was surely having fun at the sprawling swimming pool there. My driver came in and started to chat with me. His English was more 'Tanglish' with lots of Tamil words thrown in along with the strong rolling 'r' and plenty of hand gestures together with the great smile that displays sparkling white teeth that is so common to all Tamils. This really helped me understand what he wanted to convey. He wanted me to visit his home and be his guest.

I liked my driver. His name was Perumal and he was a nice guy. Honest, discreet, never said 'no' (I learned later that Indians rarely say 'no' as this is against their ethics), hardworking, always busy cleaning our car, and he was a safe driver, which was a relief considering the haphazard ways of driving here.

This terrible and frightening 'couldn't care less' attitude of driving in India is one thing I never have been able to adjust to. Some people say there are countries in the world where driving is worse than it is here, I cannot imagine how it could be worse than India.

We decided to go to Perumal's house right away. I was curious to know about his life once he finished his duty with me and I had never been to an Indian home before.

He took me through a highly populated area to his very modest one-room house covered with a thatched roof made of palm leaves, whitewashed walls, a *kollam* (a drawing in front of the houses made of rice powder meant to ward off the evil eye), and the floor was neatly washed with cow's urine. His wife folded her hands and softly said 'Namaste' as

I entered their home. I sat on a mat they unrolled and they offered me coffee made with jaggery.

Inside the home, *dhoties* (a cotton sarong worn by men), shirts, and saris were hanging on ropes or nails. In the open kitchen, which was in a corner of the only room, Perumal's wife was preparing some *puris* (puffed deep fried delicacies) and some kind of *sambar* (vegetable stew) with *dals* (lentil sauce). Smoke filled the room and it was difficult to breathe, my eyes started to water and itch. Yet, I kept smiling and indeed enjoyed what they so kindly offered me, while Perumal and his wife watched me eat. Remembering now those early days in India when I did not know the eating etiquette, I feel ashamed to have eaten with both my right and left hand, as this is not done in India. The left hand is used to clean oneself, after using the lavatory. Of course, no one had warned me of this and I was happily eating with both hands, mindless of my blunder.

They kept serving more food despite my insisting that I would not be able to eat any more.

I took leave of his wife and Perumal took me back to my Madras home. On the way back, I could still smell the smoke of the cooking fireplace and my mouth was still burning from the strong chillies I had to eat, because I did not dare leave them on my plate, nor did I dare take them out of my mouth. I thought about this man and his wife who made such a great effort to make me feel comfortable and who were so kind to me... many years later I still remember the smell of the smoke and Perumal's kindness and his wife's warm smile.

While I always thought that the French people are incapable of discipline, I discovered that Indians are the worst profiteers. They are averse to queuing and kick, push, and shove their way out, whether it is from a plane or a cinema. Indians love to play at being the cleverest ones. They cheat in games without feeling guilty about it. Petrol is sometimes mixed with kerosene, ashes with cement, water with milk, and it is better to check the change the shopkeeper hands you.

It is not only the poorest that cheat, but also the rich who never pay any income tax. At least one-third of the Indian economy is built with black money. Politicians are known to keep colossal amounts of cash in their homes. After all, India is extremely rich. Indians today must be the foremost when it comes to saving money.

Although it is slowly starting to change, up until now, most Indians had no credit cards, no shares, no bank loans, but instead saved by buying gold ornaments for women, land, and houses using *benami* (fake) names. Even small shopkeepers who sell *bidis* (small Indian cigarillos) on the street corner know how to save money. Poverty in India is the result of the tremendous upheaval of colonialism, the useless partition followed by successive political policies in the '60s, based on the Soviet model, together with immense collective inertia and resilience.

I realised that Indian people taken individually are marvellous people. They are hospitable, soft, sensitive, pleasant, and full of innate and spontaneous spirituality. The same can unfortunately not be said of the Indian masses. The gap between the rich and the poor is often shocking for a Westerner. Some Indians are so rich they could buy half of France and others are so poor that they are forced to sell their own children. Thanks to Mother Theresa, the author of the 'City of Joy', and *Slumdog Millionaire*, we are aware that Indians are often incapable of charity towards their own kin. They also have a unique version of civic sense. I experience it every day when I see them driving on Indian roads. Bus and lorry drivers here, are without a doubt amongst the most dangerous in the world. They overtake on bends or a blind hill, without even changing their gear as another lorry or overloaded bus is hurtling directly towards them from the opposite direction. The result is naturally a disaster.

Travelling by road in this country can be equated to playing Russian Roulette, especially during the night, when of course, no one bothers to lower their head lamps, or they play an off-on-off game with the lamps that leaves you completely blind for dangerous seconds while other lorries are heading straight towards you. Add to that the fact that they all use their powerful air horns all the time, even in cities. Imagine the chaos and cacophony.

How did a provincial man with Occitan roots, like me, find himself in the country of Lord Shiva?

6

LIFE IS COOL

I found that I had somehow lived a whole year in Madras. Kreglinger, my employer, had increased my salary and we moved into a very attractive colonial style home in the heart of the most posh area in Madras, with five servants to take care of our needs.

'Boy, bring a gin tonic!' an old British man was calling out to someone at the Club. A barefoot Indian wearing a turban on his head, looking very dignified with his white tunic and wide red brocade sash draped around his waist, hastened to serve us, while others were delicately placing platters full of chicken *tikkas* and other tandoori meats cooked in spices, with a light curry aroma, on our table. Next to us, the honorary Consul of Turkey was sipping a whisky soda, while his corpulent spouse was frolicking in the vast blue swimming pool of the exclusive Madras Club. He gave us a wink of complicity... every Wednesday we had the cream of

Madras society with us for dinner. My God, how beautiful life seemed to me at the time...

Our relationship with the three servants that we inherited with the new house was rather easy by then. They were charming, smiled all the time, and peppered every sentence with lots of 'Sirs', but soon enough my wife discovered that we were consuming about ten kilos of sugar per week.

'Do you drink so many cups of coffee?' my wife asked one day.

Shocked I went to the kitchen and discovered hidden in cupboards, small little packets of sugar, rice, and coffee wrapped in sheets of newspaper. The cook was taking it home at the end of the day. With the whisky I kept in a decanter on the dumbwaiter in the dining room, a different tactic was used. I was wondering what was happening to the whisky because the taste seemed to somehow diminish and change everyday. I found that the cleaning boy was helping himself to a daily shot and he refilled the decanter with the right amount of black tea to keep the level right. Even in this home, our personal privacy did not seem to be a sacred notion and the staff tended to enter our room at any odd moment. They regarded our house as their house and it did not seem to bother them if we were in the room, nor what we were doing in it.

I felt a bit out of tune with the Indians, but I was starting to appreciate their hospitality and their tolerance. In those days, neither Indian culture nor spirituality was of any interest to me. Ravi Shankar's music bored me and it didn't even cross my mind to meet my closest Indian family, or J. Krishnamurthi, the great philosopher and Indian spiritual guide admired so much by Westerners. Like most men in the '70s, I had long hair and wore bell-bottom jeans, and my wife wore miniskirts. We were right in the middle of the Hippy Era and India was our 'Kingdom'.

I was discovering India mainly during my business trips within the country, such as when I visited some parts of the Himalayas while on a business trip to Delhi to meet with a customer.

Once I decided to take a break and caught a train to Haridwar, visiting Rishikesh along the River Ganga. The place was full of foreigners seeking spirituality or *ganja* from the many sadhus waiting for them. Driving further upstream along the Alaknanda River towards the Chinese border, I discovered with awe some of the highest summits, the Nanda Devi culminating at 7816 meters, the Trishul at 7120 meters. In the early mornings, its white summits became red with the rising sun and as the hours passed, returned to blinding white again. Before nightfall, they turned pink, then orange, and lastly mauve. I still cannot find appropriate words to describe the scenery and the way one feels in a place with such strong vibrations. I understood why so many swamis came there to merge with the Ultimate, as its presence is so palpable there.

The narrow road meandered along the mountain slopes up and up, and up above the rapids of the Ganga. After Devprayag, the banks of the Alaknanda far below was scattered with the remains of vehicles, lorries, buses, jeeps, etc. — scary reminders that these were dangerous roads.

As we approached Jyoshimath, the small town where Adi Shankarananda, the famous Saint of the 8th century built his ashram, 50 km from the Chinese border, the evening turned very cold. We were as high as 3000 meters and our car was showing signs of gearbox trouble. Our driver drove us like a madman and many times, we had already had several close encounters. Even now, I wondered how we managed to get this far, allowing oncoming vehicles to pass us without driving into the abyss. I sat ahead next to the driver and my right leg began aching because I was pressing desperately on an imaginary brake.

One day I discovered Tapovanam, a small village in an incredibly beautiful valley, surrounded by high peaks and dazzling white snow, a clear dark blue sky, and hot water springs smelling of sulphur. The beauty of this place had such a fulfilling impact on me that I realised I did not need anything more from this place. I felt totally free to leave without any regrets. I went back to Madras with its heat and its miles of concrete.

The May 1968 spirit had not had much effect on me. My preoccupation was not to fix this world, but rather to feed my son and wife. Smoking grass was not my trip. I preferred a gin-tonic in the evening with expatriate friends at the very British exclusive Madras Club. So? Life was cool…

7

ROCK BOTTOM

...until 1973, when suddenly, everything collapsed. In order to promote the export of finished products such as garments, bags, shoes, etc, the Indian Government banned, without warning, the export of semi-tanned skins. I was not needed in India any longer. I was jobless, as Kreglinger had no further interest in India. They offered me a similar job in New Zealand. I hesitated, since that country did not attract me as much as India. Not that I did not like New Zealand as a country, but the climate scared me — the cold and the rain. It reminded me of the climate in Brittany, in the northwest of France. I was born a Southerner, where it is sunny most of the time and rain is sparse, a climate similar to California's. If I went back to France, I would have to go back to work in Paris — a small flat, no servant, grey sky, arrogant people running around at rush hour in the Metro. No. Not for me anymore.

Frankly speaking, my inherited Spanish pride prevented me from going back to my country defeated, a failure on a personal, and professional front. Also, I had slowly gotten attached to the people of India, despite their irritating slowness and inefficiency. It was decided. I would stay in Madras.

Gone were the servants, finished was the good life around the swimming pool of the Club, drink in hand. Finished were the parties at home where the Tout-Madras used to chat, dine, drink and dance. We had to survive on the scarce savings we had, while I looked for a way to survive, a way out of this situation.

While working in Paris, I was mixing with the fashionable crowd and learnt about fashion design through my friends. As I was good at drawing, it came to my mind to design and manufacture garments in Madras and export them to France. Any administrative work, or generally getting things done in India, takes an eternity. With each day my relationship with my wife was going from bad to worse.

One fine day, after one of our innumerable fights, she suddenly left me and my seven-year-old son for whom she would come back after six months. I had reached rock bottom. It was a total collapse. No more office, no car, no money to even pay the rent. Very often, my main meal would be a slice of bread with a sprinkle of sugar, caramelised in the toaster. I became very thin, and I was a heavy smoker then. The worst experience then was looking around the small shops on the pavements and picking up half-used cigarettes or *bidis* that cost less than one cent of our Euro. In better days, I used to smoke 60 cigarettes every day and gulp down four or five whiskies every night. Add to that the humidity and the tropical climate, and it was not a healthy lifestyle. Of course today, no alcohol or cigarettes for me at all.

Sometimes, I had the impression that I was walking on a thin wire that hardly separated me from sheer delirium. What was I doing in this country of mad people?

Why did I leave my sweet France and my darling Beziers for India, where everything was so different, so complicated, the complete antithesis of our culture? In the evenings, alone in my bedroom, I experienced an intense, unbearable loneliness. I had become so used to the never-ending natter of my wife, my son's incessant questions, and the ever-present servants who ran to me when I called. Would I end up as a beggar? Or, would I become one of those 'Mad of God', as we called those men and women who were neither beggars nor *sannyasins* (Hindu monks), whom you see on all the roads of India, dishevelled, black from dust and dirt, without goal or reason, looking at their feet while walking and talking to themselves? I actually did notice one morning in the bathroom that I was talking aloud to myself. It was imperative that I take a decision. Maybe I could go to the French Consulate in Pondicherry and pretend to have become mad and get them to repatriate me back to my country. Sometimes suicidal thoughts arose... but Lord Shiva was looking after me.

8

A LITTLE FRENCHMAN IN MADRAS

My first stroke of luck came with my meeting a Parsi gentleman, as Farsis from Persia are known in India. In the 7th century BC, the followers of Zarathustra ran away from Persia, fleeing the advance of and persecution from Islam. They found refuge and freedom to practise their faith in India, as the Indian rulers were tolerant of new religions.

Rahul Batliwalla was a smooth talker and a womaniser (especially if there was white skin under the skirt) and he had a wide network of contacts, but not much money. He had the intelligence to spot the potential I had in me and he could foresee what he could get out of me, as I had enthusiasm and was hardworking, although I was slightly messy. We formed a company and called it Fabratel. With a small amount of money my mother sent me, we bought five stitching machines, scissors and thread — the minimum one needs to start working with and I created my first little 'at home' collection.

A second stroke of luck came my way and I grabbed it. Having heard about me, a buyer from Au Printemps, a famous department store in Paris, came to see me. I showed her my small collection and she was impressed with what she saw.

She then asked me to take her to our factory, thinking it was in the same building. In fact we had no such thing as a factory, and I was scared to frighten her away if I admitted this to her, so I bluffed.

'Our factory is not here, since it is quite big. We established it in the outskirts of Madras, about 40 km away.'

It was May and very hot (about 42°C) and she was already sweating profusely. She immediately said, 'Oh my God, 40 km in this heat! I just can't go there! I can't bear this heat and humidity... No problem, we trust you have the right tools to work with.'

They placed a very substantial order with us, the first in a long series, as we would work together for the next nine years… till Fabratel lasted.

Where were we going to find the money to make so many pieces? 15,000! My partner started hunting for a bank that would agree to finance us against an irrevocable letter of credit from the customer. We got it and immediately started to look for a suitable place to put up our machines, stock, and office. While I sweated it out like a donkey, my partner was having a good time at the Club, entertaining all the girls he could lay his eyes on.

Those days were just the beginning of outsourcing and thanks to the influence of Au Printemps, who was passing information to similar European stores, the word of mouth tactic started to pay off and pay off very well indeed. People heard that in Madras was a little Frenchman who could make a nice low-priced collection.

So, while Rahul was having a grand time gallivanting at the Club, I was catching my overcrowded morning bus at 8 a.m. to go and open our factory/office, that was if the bus would even deign to stop and pick me up. Most of the time, the buses were completely packed and usually leaned dangerously to the side of the footboard from where I was hanging precariously while holding on to a window rail. I had no car or bike. It was the same scenario on the way back in the evening when my 'day' ended at around 9.30-10 p.m.

I worked the whole day in a damp over-heated place with fans pushing down the even hotter air from the corrugated metallic roof. I took care of almost everything except the writing of cheques. Designing, supervising the preparation of the collection, selecting fabric, selecting personnel, supervising the production, keeping contact with our customers, and even looking after the paperwork, which was the most difficult task of all — to negotiate with the Indian government and get things done without paying a paisa (one cent of a rupee) as bribe.

Meanwhile, I had enough money to buy cigarettes, as Rahul was giving me a royal amount of Rs. 1500 (about 30 Euros), nothing more than a pittance. On arriving home, I could down my usual four or five whiskies and fall asleep utterly exhausted to start all over again in the morning.

I was not satisfied with the way our foreign customers were taking us for a ride as though we were their slaves. I could see that India was a great country with an even greater potential and was a huge upcoming market that we should tap into. It was here that 'things' would happen and not in the 'Old World'. Therefore, I asked my associate to look for a place where we could set up our store to sell our men's shirts. He found a shop in the only five-star hotel in Madras in those days (circa 1977), the Taj Coromandel. It was not a grand store as such, but certainly, it was a good start, as this was the only happening place in Chennai.

It attracted many people from the 'Jet Set' and very well known Kollywood actors became our regular customers. As I was the designer, it encouraged me to know that many celebrities came to buy my creations.

My mother came to visit me in India. Her friends in France tried to dissuade her from undertaking such a trip. They told her, 'You are mad at your age to travel to a country of savages, and wild animals, and it is so hot.'

She answered, 'If my son is there, then I can be there too.'

By this time, I had upgraded to riding a scooter, which I had to kick at least 15 times before it would start. My mother did not say anything and would come with me, riding pillion. It was the monsoon and the roads were flooded. The sewage system in Madras is poor and cannot carry away so much water. But, I had to go to my factory because we had deliveries to complete. My mother refused to stay at home waiting for me and she wanted to sit behind me on that stubborn scooter, that took a long time to start and we would go through wheel-deep murky water, while it poured down heavily. She brought her knitting and crochet and would sit comfortably and make coasters for my house. From time to time, she would go to the assembly unit to see what was happening. Her knowledge of garment manufacturing was still very sharp and often she would come back from her factory floor visit and tell me what was happening. One evening she said, 'You better go and see what is happening there. They are assembling the sleeves on the wrong side.' Usually she was right.

Despite the good orders we were getting, I was not feeling well in my skin. I missed my wife and son and it was clear to me that my Parsi friend was taking advantage of me.

I was also not satisfied with our store in the Taj, although we were clothing the rich and famous. I wanted my brand to be more popular. I asked my associate to develop our brand by opening more stores in the good areas of Madras and later also in Bombay, but he was a man without vision and did not agree. He was concentrating only on acting in stage plays, writing poems, and running after every white expatriate woman coming his way.

9

SHIVASHAKTI

In 1983, I dropped my Parsi partner and left along with Jayapal, one of the staff who had become my friend. We formed a company we called Shivashakti and started again from scratch with nothing in the pocket except a few machines and some equipment, in a country that was irritating me as much as it was fascinating me.

Jayapal's family was very poor and I was not rich at all. We did not have sufficient money to set up a proper factory. We hired a bungalow and put all my personal furniture in one room, set up one room as our office, used another room for stock and the big hall, which would normally be used as a sitting room, was used for cutting and garmenting with 20 machines and a cutting table. We installed pictures of Lord Ganesh and prayed for the best. We struggled hard to rise out of this situation. Once again, I was back to starving.

We had no money and again my mother helped me. There was no question about us wasting this help. As for food, we survived on instant food. 'Thank you Nestle for giving us Maggi Noodles,' we murmured during meal times, because that was what we lived on. It was fast to make and cheap to buy.

We started working for a Swiss friend of ours who had a big store in Basel. I designed the garments and we made them in our own unit. We had to go to Switzerland often and we used to spend about four months of the year there. I loved that place and we picked up a bit of German during our stay there. Our lodging in Basel was special. Our Swiss friend's father owned many companies and one of them was in real estate. He gave us an apartment in a dilapidated building and we had to content ourselves with bad second-hand furniture that our friend collected from dumping yards.

Not that his family was not rich, they were, but he did not want to depend on his father and did not see the need to buy anything, as everything, according to him, was available on the pavements of Basel, where on specific days, the population dumped furniture they did not want any more. Of course, some were not usable at all, but others were good and with a little repair could be used for another ten years. Our Swiss friend was not very interested in cleanliness and that was difficult for me to digest and accept.

Although our financial situation was more comfortable, I was heading straight towards a nervous breakdown. I was approaching my fifties, the smoking and the evening whiskies were becoming more and more difficult for my body to bear.

Back at home in Chennai, at night, in my narrow, over-heated small bedroom, rats ran over my body. The same questions arose once again — what the hell am I doing here?

For whom and for what purpose was I making all this effort? Like so many Westerners in India, would I become a failure and end up a wreck?

This time, the Ultimate one sent me a sign, a real one.

10

RAJI OPENS THE DOOR

I had Brahmin neighbours, the priest caste of the traditional Hindu hierarchy, still found today at all levels of the Indian society. A Brahmin lady caught my attention. From the balcony of my house, I admired the way she tucked her sari between her legs to run after her son whom she was teaching to ride a cycle. We soon started to make conversation. Raji had married a Pakistani Sindhi some time ago. This was not allowed under the caste system as he was an outcast and she had eloped from her father's home. Many years later, her father had forgiven her and asked her to return home, which she had done. She invited me to their home and while I was enjoying *idlis* (steamed rice and white lentil dumplings) that she offered me, she talked to me about spirituality, Pranayama (breathing exercises), and meditation as a remedy for my depressed mood. I had been living in India for nearly 15 years by then, and this was the first time that somebody was talking to me about spirituality, and I liked it.

Raji, and her father, who was always present during our meetings, gave me a book, *The Gospel of Paramahamsa Ramakrishna.* She told me, 'Ramakrishna was a man who did not know how to read or write, but his inner strength was so great, the truth emanating from him was so powerful that the whole of India used to come to meet him. Learned people, illiterates, the poor and the rich, Brahmins and *shudras* (untouchables) flocked to the Temple of Dakshineshwar, by the Hooghly River near Calcutta, to prostrate themselves at the feet of the greatest sage of the 19th century.'

In the evening, back in my flat, under a bare bulb, I opened the book and read the first few words, 'God is in all men, but all men are not in God. That is why they suffer.'

In a flash, I had a sudden understanding, the intuitive revelation, of what India is and the treasure next to which I had been living for so many years. Later on, I could understand Ramakrishna's words, which had moved me so much, he had everything, though he owned nothing.

He was poor and illiterate, but he had great wisdom, was full of love, and full of goodness. I was discovering that in spite of having lost my wife, my child, job, friends, and even having almost lost my mind, I owned everything in the bottom of my heart — so present, so warm, and so close. I had been feeling a great void in me and after I finished reading this book, I intuitively realised that the truth was not outside of me, in the material world, but rather inside myself. What joy I felt! I had found the real meaning of living, the reason to live, to get to know oneself, to find one's goal, one's aim.

So much time was lost already!

Within a month, Raji introduced me to the main Indian sacred texts. The *Mahabarata*, which weaves in a grand scale not yet surpassed, the epic of the soul of India, the customs and practices of India, as well as its cultural, political, and social life and the second great Indian epic poem in a similar spirit, the *Ramayana.*

I also discovered the *Bhagavad-Gita.* According to me, it contains everything that every Indian, indeed every human being, needs and should know to live a meaningful life. The answers to all questions humanity needs to learn are in this book. It is in this sacred text that one can find these illuminating words, 'One does not work for results, but rather in a selfless manner, this is Dharma.'

Yes, Dharma (the principle of righteousness) is what helped me become conscious of my real inner ME.

The Little Frenchman from Beziers was devouring anything and everything that could give him more information. I suddenly had a fever for knowledge. Raji also introduced me to *bhajans*, ancient hymns that all faithful Hindus chant in honour of God. This was yet another revelation, I have always liked the magical rhythms and incantatory intonations of Gregorian singing, and like with the hymns, I had the same experience when I heard *bhajans*, which also felt familiar to me, as if I already knew them.

11

THESE THOUGHTS ARE NOT YOURS

I ended all my bad habits, including cigarettes (I had started to spit up black phlegm after endless bouts of coughing), whiskies, the *ganja* I had started to smoke from time to time, and I also stopped eating all kinds of meat. I became a vegetarian and started my initiation into Hatha yoga practices. My teacher was Swami Vedananda. He taught us such valuable lessons at no charge at all, which is almost unheard of today. He said, 'My aim is to bring lost souls to Spirituality'. The very first thing he taught me was the meaning of the word 'yoga', which is 'union'. The word does not only pertain to Hatha yoga, the body yoga, as Westerners usually believe. He told me that there are many kinds of yoga. Karma yoga is the yoga of work and action, Jnana yoga is the yoga of knowledge, Bhakti yoga is the yoga of devotion and of course, Hatha yoga. Behind all these types of yogas, there is Lord Shiva, The Supreme Reality.

Step by step, my Swami led me to discover Lord Shiva. 'Do not consider Lord Shiva as a God, think of Shiva as Space with a big 'S', and imagine that Lord Shiva is present in each and every atom that makes up your body, the air you breathe, the whole of the Universe, in each creature, each plant, and each stone also.'

He gave me a philosophical treatise to read, I appreciated the fact that it explained the creation of the Universe in a way that sounded logical to me. It, the Ultimate Consciousness, is the starting point of space and time and spreads outwards in all directions from this centre.

Catholic by birth, Cartesian by my French conditioning, one can imagine my state of mind concerning joining a spiritual system so alien to me. Of course, I had also heard how harmful some sects and Gurus could be, therefore, I was treading very carefully on a path that could lead to such unknown discoveries. However, I felt confident about my destiny and judgment.

Then came the time for meditation. What a big word 'meditation' is, as it conjures up images of things mystical and the practices of initiated, learned people.

'Not at all,' answered Swamiji. 'It is a very rational science, which can be practised by anyone, anytime, and anywhere. This is what will allow you to look inside yourself, because meditation allows you to interiorise, it brings us into contact with the best of our Self, and allows us to discover our real Self.'

I learnt that in India there are hundreds of ways to meditate and feel different effects. Swami taught me one of them, 'Learn to dissociate from your thoughts and let them come and go within your mind, without attaching any importance to them, without following any of them.'

The first time I tried his advice, it was no good at all. The more I tried not to follow any single thought, the more the thoughts would rush at me and insist that I follow this one and that one and all my problems, personal, and professional were rushing at me and calling for attention. Swami Vedananda told me patiently, 'Up until now you were the one who was pulling the cart and the bulls were sitting behind you driving the cart! They represent the mind (your thoughts). Now, try to reverse the situation. For this you should not force your mind or stop your thoughts. Act as though these thoughts are not yours and let them pass.'

It took me a whole year of meditation, before I found to my surprise that my mind had quietened and my thoughts were getting disciplined to a certain extent. This had an immediate effect on my personality. Since the time my wife had left me, I had become a man prone to violent bursts of anger. I used to bang doors so firmly that the plaster and paint around them would crack and fall down. Thanks to meditation, my nervous system started to relax and my bouts of anger became less and less frequent. I also noticed that my concentration and my capacity to work multiplied.

12

MALABAR COAST

After some time, I could see that our Swiss friend was not interested in expanding his business further to other cities in Switzerland and was content with his living conditions and what he had. His father was financing him and I was not sure how much longer he would be patient and pour money into his son's endeavours. I decided that I had had enough and that Jayapalan and I had better look out for an alternative direction if we wanted to progress beyond living with cast-off furniture and Maggi noodles. We stopped our business with our Swiss friend and parted as good friends.

A bleak future stared us in the face and once again, I was back to square one. I had to rack my brain and quickly find a way out of yet another dead-end in order to move forward. Starting a whole new brand requires making a full collection of products — shirts, t-shirts, jeans, etc. It would be a difficult affair for Jayapal and me to get all the funds we required to finance such a project.

Then I thought I could at least create a line of men's shirts. Only shirts. Only one model, with two options — long sleeves, or short sleeves. We would offer them in a variety of hand-woven fabrics.

Before embarking on such a new adventure — I call this an adventure, because we had no experience in directly selling to multi-brand stores — we had to find a way to sell them, so that the stores would be interested. At what price should we sell them? So many questions presented themselves. We had to find a French salesman who would be interested in being our representative to sell to the stores. Secondly, we had to make a little sample collection for the sales representative to show to the storeowners and to get orders. If they liked our products, then surely I could find a way out and get the shirts made once we had orders in hand.

Now, we had to choose a brand name for the shirts. While reading about South India, I had come across the word 'Malabar', which was the name of the people living in the state of Kerala, South India. It also happens to be a French word, which means 'strong man, muscle man'. It was an original and ideal name. I designed the label 'Malabar Coast', and had it woven and stitched on our products.

When my little collection of 20 shirts made in a wide variety of fabric and colours was ready, I bought an economy class plane ticket and carried them to France. There, with the help of some old school friends, I was introduced to a couple who were interested in buying my collection. They liked the general idea and the selection of fabric and colours. As it was a direct business, from the Indian manufacturer (ourselves) to the storeowner, with the sales representative as the only intermediary, I could offer attractive wholesale prices. We waited anxiously for the results.

After about two months of roaming the south of France from Toulouse to Marseille to Valence, we had gathered orders of about 20,000 pieces to be dispatched within three months, to a list of French customers. We were delighted; as indeed, it was not a small first time order.

Of course, a big question immediately sprang up — where were we going to get money to purchase the fabric and pay for the making and shipping of the shirts, the customs duty, taxes, etc? How were we going to get the import license to clear the goods in France? Who would dispatch the shirts to the customers once they got to France, and how? How was I going to get paid? And many more questions. Most importantly, we didn't have enough money to start with as my mother's previous contribution was dwindling rapidly.

I had to meet my French banker. I had no other way left but to knock on his door. Of course, it is well known that a bank gives you an umbrella when the sun shines brightly and takes it back once it starts to rain. I had to do a lot of convincing to a get a little help from him, on the express condition that I bring collateral. Since I owned nothing, I had to ask my mother once again for help. After consulting my brothers and sister, she agreed to mortgage our home as a guarantee. The deal with the banker was that once the goods were billed to our customers, I could discount their promissory note and avail of their value immediately. It was indeed a breather for us. If, however, my customers failed to pay on the stipulated date on the promissory note they had signed, the amount given by the bank would be reversed and they would debit from my account.

With the bank's Damocles' sword hanging over my head and since I was somewhat happy to have found a way out of this financial situation, I embarked on manufacturing the orders. Time was flying by and we had to deliver on time. For this, I rushed back to Madras and started working. We needed more than 20 different fabrics and I rushed from one corner of India to another as we had no computers in those days and a telephone call was not the right way to book fabric. I also needed to see the weavers and check the quality of the cloth.

We had moved to a better place, a little far from the city centre. It was a colony built by the Indian Army for its retired officers and had the advantage of a clean environment, ample clean water, a reasonable rent, and nice decent neighbours. We had sold our Ambassador car, and Jayapal bought a second-hand bike and I had a second-hand moped, which regularly let me down. We could not afford anything more comfortable and reliable at the time. We rented two houses in the same street, hardly 100 meters away from one another. One was used as our office-cum-factory and the other was our residence. It reduced our travelling expenses and commute time substantially.

Swami Vedananda, my yoga teacher, lived on the other side of the city and I had to set off when it was still night in order to reach his place at around 5.30 am. My moped was strangely okay when it had to take me there, and I don't know why, but it regularly gave up on me when we were halfway home. I would kick the starter repeatedly, but to no avail, I had to push it all the way back and would reach our house completely soaked in sweat and dead tired.

We finally managed to ship our orders on time after lots of problems and worries. Now, I had to rush back to France to receive the goods, to do the paperwork for the import licenses, clear the goods from the customs and bring them to the little warehouse I had rented especially on the outskirts of Beziers, in the south of France. I had to unpack, check the quality again, repack them according to each customer's order and personally deliver the parcels. I had to drive as far as Lille, near the Belgium border, 1000 km away from Beziers. I could not use the motorways, as I could not afford to pay the toll fees, so this lengthened each delivery time and the distance I had to drive. I had no choice but to keep a strict watch on expenses. I drove long distances through the night, so that I would reach the destination in the morning when the stores opened for the day. I would return the same day, as I could not afford to pay for one night's lodging. Sometimes, deadbeat, I would stop by the side of the road and sleep in the car.

Now, that the deliveries were made, I was anxious for the customers to pay me. All our payments were made at the end of every 60 days, which meant I planned to receive all the money at least 90 days after delivery. In the meantime, I had to create the next collection for the next season. Since the sales representative was good the first time around, he wanted to have the new collection as soon as possible so that he could visit even more customers and expand our sales areas. Therefore, I had no other way but to go back to Madras immediately and start working on new designs. Although the sales representative had promised me that he would make sure the customers' payments were made promptly, he didn't and in order not to be in the soup with my bankers, I caught a plane and rushed back to France to activate their payments. There, I learnt that three of our biggest customers had gone bankrupt, and since we were their smallest debtor, we were told we had very little chance of getting our money. We never did get it.

Though some of our customers paid us on time, the rest were hard to push when it came to paying their dues. Of course, by this time, the time limit of their promissory notes at the bank had elapsed and the bank debited my account, with interest running and piling up. To avoid losing her home, my mother gave me her savings to bring back our French bank account to a healthier level. Meanwhile, I was running from one store to the other, trying to corner the owners for money owed to us.

They couldn't say anything critical about the products, as they had sold everything. They knew I spent most of my time in India and our sales representative was not very pushy, so they thought they could get away without paying us, but I was watching them closely.

Once, I had to recover dues from a store in Ales, southern France. I started early from Beziers and once in town, I parked my car at a distance and walked to the shop. I saw only the saleswoman inside. I entered the shop and asked for the boss. With a sad smile, she said, 'He saw you coming and ran out the back door. You will find him there at the café up the street. He is waiting for you to leave town.'

I came out of the store fuming and walked off in the direction opposite to the café. I walked in a big circle and reached the café without being seen by the owner of the store who was peacefully enjoying his *pastis* and watching the street near his store. Stunned, he saw me entering from the opposite direction; I had caught him unaware. I demanded my payment loudly. Everyone in the café was listening and watching what was going on. I insisted he pay me immediately, which he did. Without a word, he wrote me a cheque. I would not have left him without his cheque in my pocket anyway. It took so much effort to get this payment and I had to work hard to get our dues from many other storeowners also.

I spent most of that stay in France trying to recover payments as best as I could. I was not however, able to recover payments from the three bankrupt companies and their orders amounted to the biggest quantities. This killed our short-lived, painful adventure with our own brand in France. My mother lost a lot of money on my account and I was not able to generate enough profit to finance the next collection. I did not even have enough funds to purchase a return ticket to Madras. I felt stressed out to the core, dejected, useless, worn out and without any idea about how to start the next collection. It was the end of the road for us, once again.

Late one afternoon, I went to my friends in Beziers — Gerard and Helene Ratiney. I was in tears as I told them the situation. I didn't know where and whom to turn to. I was a mess. For the first time, I really had doubts about my ability to succeed and come out of this difficult situation. Of course, I couldn't ask Gerard and Helene to help me financially as they were not rich enough to lend me the amount I needed.

My French bank, would not lend me any more funds till I cleared my debt to them, and the interest was piling up daily. I fell silent, sitting on their sofa. I heard them talking softly to each other and could not understand what they were saying.

Then they said to me, 'Christian, what about us?'

I did not understand their question.

'What about you, what?' I replied.

'Yes, why don't you ask us if we could help you?'

'How can you help me with the salaries of a teacher in a government school and a nurse?' I asked.

'Yes, we are far from rich. However, we can ask Bank X to give us a loan and since we are civil servants, we get it at a preferential interest rate. You will have to repay the principal and the low interest rate. That's all.'

I could not believe my ears! You cannot imagine how I felt... suddenly, the weight on my shoulders felt so light. I could not control the tears welling up in my eyes.

The personal loan was processed quickly by the bank and I could have it in my own account quite quickly. I purchased a ticket and rushed back to India as I had the seed of a plan in the back of my mind that should enable us this time, to come out of the poverty that Jayapal and I seemed to be destined to remain in, and that we so desperately were trying to get out of.

Even a name for the new business came to me — 'Fashions International'.

13

FIVE SECONDS FOR ETERNITY

Swami Vedananda decided that after two years of *sadhana* (spiritual practice), I was ready for the next step and he invited me to accompany him to meet his own Guru, Swami Sarveswara, who lived 200 km south of Madras, and 150 km from Salem, near the city of Tiruchirapalli. After a bumpy, seemingly endless four-hour journey in a packed, uncomfortable, and dirty bus, we arrived at Ullundurpettai, a very small, crowded, dusty little town, which seemed to have been built in a hurry, without any order or aesthetic sense. Exhausted, I was wondering again, what I was doing here on the other side of the world.

In a new area of the town, there were empty plots and a few houses, which seemed unfinished. We knocked on the door.

'Wait,' answered a voice in Tamil from the inside.

Swami Vedananda smiled. 'He is covering himself.'

Finally, we were let into a small empty room with not a single piece of furniture, behind the Guru were three pictures of Lord Shiva in different postures, on his left a brass *trishul* (tri-fork), and in front of him were incense sticks stuck into a banana and small packets of *prasadam* (food offered to Gods, sanctified in a temple, and given to devotees).

He was wearing two orange *dhoties* (cotton cloths), one covering his chest and the other wrapped around his waist and hiding his folded legs. He didn't look at us but with a grunt, directed us to sit in front of him, on the floor, like him.

The first thing that shocked me was when I noticed stumps instead of his hands and feet! Swami Vedananda had not told me that Swami Sarveswara had leprosy and had neither hands nor feet!

The second shock was when he said, without looking at me, 'I was waiting for you.'

I couldn't believe my ears. What was he telling me? How could he have known about me? There was no telephone here. The Guru had not yet finished astonishing me.

'You are living your thirteenth and last life, but it is not the first time that you have reincarnated in India...'

'What does he mean?' I asked Swami Vedananda.

The Guru did not answer my question, but instead asked, 'Why did you come here?'

I answered, 'I am looking for peace. Peace of the mind, peace of the heart.'

He grunted in reply, 'You need only five seconds. Five seconds and you will have understood everything. The whys of Life, the hows of this existence, the reason for our sufferings... the veil of Maya (ignorance) will tear apart for you.'

He looked at me again and touching his chest with his stump, he announced.

'It is here in your heart (pause)... not in your head... everything is all inside.'

He then suddenly looked me straight in the eyes and I felt a wave of affection, a wave of love, compassion, and tenderness. That look, what intensity, what beauty!

'You will get those five seconds in your Life. You have your five seconds in your heart.'

He turned to Swami Vedananda and told him, 'Spiritually speaking he is 100 years old, but he has not yet got his five seconds.'

He looked at me intently and told me, 'You were born for India. It is possible that you came out of India. However, you will always come back here... One day you will be very famous.'

Me? Known? He must be joking.

Then with a sign of the head to Swami Vedananda, the meeting was over. For the last time my Guru smiled at me, full of kindness, full of affection, he seemed to be saying good-bye, or rather, '*au revoir*'.

Swami Vedananda prostrated himself in front of his leper Guru. As instructed by Swami Vedananda, I also timidly prostrated myself in front of this strange yet very affectionate man. I was deeply shaken, astounded, and moved. Swami Vedananda and I went back to Madras, four hours on a rickety bus driven on a road full of potholes. Something like a mantra sang inside me for a while.

'Five seconds for eternity… five seconds for eternity… five seconds for eternity...'

14

YOU ARE SHIVA AND NOTHING ELSE

From then on, every weekend, after having worked hard the whole week, I would go back to Swami Sarveswara, four to five hours of a stressful bus ride. At the end of the day, spent from talking in my broken Tamil with him, after a meagre dinner, I would fall asleep, exhausted from the journey, the heat and the sticky humidity. Lying on a mat on the floor of the veranda, without a mosquito net, the heat, the mosquitoes, the hours on the bus... one needed to have faith in this man.

Sometimes I had doubts. Who is this man? What does he want from me? Has he really got powers? One day in May, Guruji (an affectionate way of calling one's Guru), seemed to sense that I needed more proof, so he asked me, 'Do you feel hot?'

I answered, 'Yes.'

'Go to rest, it will rain at 5 p.m. this afternoon.'

Monsoon would arrive only in August and the sky that day was a washed out blue with not a single cloud to be seen. What was he talking about?

At 5 p.m. it poured, and it became much cooler. I went back to see him, and he asked, 'Are you feeling cool enough now?'

I was astounded. How could he have known about the rains when there was not a cloud in the sky a few hours ago? He did not have a TV or a newspaper to look at the weather forecast for the day. How could a man, without hands and feet, hopeless, and without a future, living in such a sordid environment, living with a mutilated body, be so beautiful, so happy, and so calm?

'What is it you want?' asked the Guru.

'I want to know who I am, and why I am on this Earth.'

The Guru remained silent for an instant, and then looked at me, looking straight into my eyes, said 'You are Shiva and nothing else.'

Once again, I remained dumbfounded. I remember having read the definition of who Lord Shiva is. He is All. He is the atoms and the particles that form the atoms.

He is the Space in between those particles. He is the Energy that makes those particles move, keeping them together. He is the Gravity that rules All that is seen and unseen or yet to be seen. He is Time. He is All that Is and Is Not. In fact, using a pronoun that defines the gender is not appropriate. He is It. He is masculine. He is feminine. He is neither one nor the other. He is Both and He is none. We call it Brahman.

I also remembered the meaning of a Shiva Lingam. It is not an anthropomorphic representation, but a cylindrical shape that shows Its Infinity, because a circle has neither a beginning nor end. If men are temporal, the Ultimate cannot have any form — hence It is All the forms and the formless. Therefore, the Shiva Lingam contains the All and the All is contained in It. You can measure the Lingam, but you cannot measure what is *in* it.

Every Saturday, I would sit next to the one I now considered my Guru and I would listen to him speak. Sometimes it was enough just to be seated next to him, without him uttering a word, for my thoughts to calm down, so that I could feel Peace coming into me, overtaking me.

Besides the unbearable heat, the painful bus rides, the mosquitoes, the exhausting discomfort, my rational and Cartesian mind would time after time rebel. Was Swami Sarveswara trying to brainwash me?

He never asked me for either money or gifts. Little by little, I was discovering around him a kind of aura, a wisdom I could not explain. However, I was not yet ready to accept everything from him. One day he told me, 'Next Friday, during Amavasai (No Moon day), at 6 p.m., you will go to the Vriduchallam Temple, north of Trichy.'

15

MY LIFE CHANGES

The Temple of Vriduchallam is a very ancient Shivaite sanctuary. 'Many yogis have come to meditate here', murmurs Swami Vedananda. In the Sanctum Sanctorum, a Shiva Lingam was shining in the dark. As in the style of many Tamil Nadu temples, we entered an inside courtyard with a covered corridor around it where there are small recesses with statues depicting various representations of Lord Shiva. It was the time when the faithful came to pray and, as usual, this happens in an informal manner, men sitting on the ground in a corner were loudly discussing something and women were vociferously chanting ancient Tamil prayers, all unmindful of the *pujaris* (priests) who were violently shaking bells. It was as though no one cared about what they were doing and no one cared about my presence either. I, a *dorai* (white skinned man), was lost in this crowd, witnessing a scenario that hasn't changed in millennia.

Swami Vedananda asked me to sit in front of the main Shiva Lingam, which had two smaller lingams on either side, and told me to meditate. I closed my eyes, but I was exhausted. It was hot in the middle of May. We had travelled by bus, which did not have air-conditioning, plus the long walk under the scorching sun on a dusty road to reach the temple had sapped me of all my energy.

Drenched in perspiration, I felt drained. Immediately a flood of thoughts invaded my mind. "What am I doing here? Have I lost my head? Is it all only a dream?" I painfully tried to harness my mind and prevent it from hooking onto any of the thoughts flying by, as I had been taught. At first, I felt as though I would never succeed and started chanting in my mind 'Aum Namah Shivaya', a mantra, which my Guru had taught me privately by whispering it in my ear for this occasion. Then little by little, the noises started to fade away, even though part of me was still aware that I was not alone there. Then my thoughts steadily began to fade, and my mental landscape emptied perceptibly.

As taught by Swami Vedananda, I first brought my mind to a single luminous point — the Psychic centre. Soon, I felt an internal warmth overtaking me with the sense of a weightless body and this luminous point slowly moved up and fixed itself between my eyes, the place that Hindus call the third eye and which is the location of one of the most important *chakras* (centre of energy). Then, my personal self disappeared into the background and I felt everything falling into place.

At that moment, I had completely lost consciousness of my body and did not even feel the drops of sweat that ran down my forehead. I only faintly felt my slow rhythmic breathing, which after some time completely disappeared and I sat there, in front of the Shiva Lingam, suspended in time and space.

Suddenly, I felt a strong presence there in front of me. It is impossible to define exactly what this presence was and I did not even try to reason.

An immense compassion, ineffable joy, an inexpressible oneness, filled me up. All my pains, worries, mental wounds, all my anguish seemed to take second place as far as priorities go. 'You are Lord Shiva,' my Guruji had told me.

Some time passed in that second state, I was unaware of time or space or the heat and noise. I could not see anything of what was happening around me. I perceived a bright light emerging from the darkness, which seemed to slowly melt back into darkness and then the shape of an enormous Shiva Lingam came to me, surrounded with sparkling blinding flames and covered with white flowers and a *puttu* (third eye) across it. Not a sound, total silence, a feeling of perfect purity and most importantly an Infinite Power, an Omnipresent Being overtook me.

I had no idea how long this experience lasted, for a fraction of an instant, one hour, a day, a year, or no time at all? I felt a hand gently rest on my shoulder.

I opened my eyes slowly and I saw that it was night. I tried to stand up, but my legs were completely numb. I couldn't move at all. I looked at my watch and it was 8.30 p.m. We had reached the temple at 4.30 p.m., so it meant that I had sat on this hard granite surface for nearly four hours, totally cut off from the outside world. My body had been insensitive to pain all this while... Aum Namah Shivaya... had I seen Lord Shiva?

During the bus ride back to Chennai, I tried to analyse what had happened to me, what was that experience which was now so present in me. Maybe the heavy reading and thinking about Lord Shiva that I had been doing the month before had made me susceptible? Maybe it was my Guru's influence? Lord Shiva may be only a human transcription of the formless, without any attributes.

Thinking about it, I understood that neither a masculine nor a feminine element is attributed to the Shiva Lingam and yet it contained both. I was lost in my Cartesian reasoning, but I did know that after many years, I now had touched something at the very root of my Being.

Swami Vedananda asked me what happened during my meditation but I couldn't and didn't want to tell him at the time. Only a few days after my return to Chennai, could I talk to him about it and he decided that we should go and see Guruji again.

16

HE/SHE/IT

At Swami Sarveswara's modest home, I related my Shiva Lingam experience. The leper Guru smiled.

'Why do you think I sent you there? You must keep that experience in your heart and never should you forget it, because many wish to have such an experience, but very few get it. Only few can see what you saw...'

I was flabbergasted. How could I have been singled out? Me, an ordinary man who not long ago was sure he had reached rock-bottom, whose inability to control his life caused him to feel as if he was drifting into a dark bottomless pit. Since then, this vision of a Shiva Lingam with pure white flowers and flames keeps on coming back to me without warning. Each time I feel the same beatitude, comfort, the same feeling of having found the aim and meaning of my life. It recharges me acting like powerful batteries and gives purpose to my life. The experience itself has become more important than the vision and has never left me. Maybe it is 'that' which I transmit involuntarily to others.

At the time, lots of questions clashed with one another to find answers in my boiling brain. 'Who is Shiva? Why did I feel a feminine presence as well as a masculine one?'

My Guru explained, 'Shiva is the Intention to do and Shakti is the element of Creation that acts on the impulse of the Intention. There is no Shiva without Shakti. Shiva is the masculine element and Shakti is the feminine element. Therefore, there cannot be any action without the intention to act and vice-versa.'

I remembered that Shiva is also Ardhanareswara, half-male and half-female and neither male nor female, and not neutral either!

Sri Aurobindo had said, 'Without Him nothing happens. Without Her nothing happens.'

My Guru continued, 'The cylinder of the Lingam symbolises the imaginary limits in you of what is Known in the inside and of what is yet to be Known outside of that cylinder. In fact, both merge into one. What you need to know is already within you. One learns only what one has inside of oneself already, from which comes the Shivaite saying, 'I am This, but also That. I am this one, however, I am that one too.'

I must have looked puzzled, because he began to explain patiently to me.

'Lord Shiva is beyond shapes, he is the Auspicious One, the one who is good, not the Destroyer of the Hindu mythology — Rudra. Love is the first quality.'

My Guru added, 'I feel His Presence constantly in me, within and without, in me and in others. I am communing with Him/Her/It all the time. I do not need dogmas or rituals, as God is everywhere all the time. Hence, we have no need for masses, or *pujas*, or rituals. 'I' is Shiva, 'He' or 'She' is also Shiva, 'It' is also Shiva. Shiva is the Ultimate, the Absolute, the Absolute Energy, and the Imminent. He/She/It is not limited by Space, Shapes, or Time. He is the naked mendicant.

'He is the King dressed in gold ornaments, He is the newborn child and He is the old man bent over his cane. Buddha is Shiva, Christ is Shiva, Krishna is Shiva, and Allah is Shiva...'

Later on, I would learn that this is Hindu tolerance, to accept all religions and understand that one can reach God by many paths. The world thinks that Hinduism is a polytheistic religion; in fact, Hinduism is the most monotheistic religion in the world because it recognises the uniqueness of the one, the Creator, in the multitude and in between it. It is with a multiplicity of views that Indian seers and sages understood the multiplicity of the unknowable, which is a transcendent reality.

17

COVERED BY THE FOUR WINDS

Six months later, during one of our usual meetings at his place in Ullundurpettai, Swami Sarveswara told me, 'You are ready for *Sannyas Diksha* (the initiation for becoming a monk).'

I immediately said yes, without thinking. As preparation, he recommended that I take a trip to Varanasi (old Benares), the ancient holy city of Bharat (as India was known) to live as a *sannyasin* (Hindu monk). There I slept on the *ghats* (steps along the Ganges), ate with the *sadhus* (ascetics), bathed in the Ganges and practised the daily *sadhana* (spiritual practices) as instructed by my Guru. In the beginning, it was rather hard.

On the first day, I noticed shapeless sacks covered with multicoloured cloth lined up side by side, swarming with flies, which would take off in a frenzy whenever someone came too close to it. I then realised that the sacks contained dead bodies that had been brought there for burning and to be thrown into the Ganges.

It was meant to stop the terrible cycle of re-birth. Indian people bring their relatives from afar to be cremated in this spot, hence the incredible number of sacks. One could often see dusty jeeps converging towards Benares from all corners of India, carrying their colourful loads with shiny ribbons along the border floating in the wind.

After experiencing the vision of Lord Shiva, should my life not change completely? Why should I bother working in this rag trade? All this belonged to the past and I was prepared to clear the table of my past completely and leave this brutal, aggressive, materialistic world, and as a swami, devote myself completely to a spiritual life.

January 26, 1988 was the day of my Sannyas Diksha. In a little room in my Guruji's home, I undressed. Guruji had my clothes taken away and started to perform a special *puja* of my death, which he followed with another *puja* for my re-birth as Swami Pranavananda Brahmendra Avadhuta (The Liberated One).

After the ceremony, he asked me to come close to him and he whispered another mantra into my ear, which I still chant regularly and am not allowed to share with anyone. He gave me a set of two *dhoties* earthen orange in colour. Guruji asked me to dress up again and told me, 'You should always wear these *dhoties* and we shall show you how to fold them.

One is to cover your chest and the other to cover your private parts and legs. Whenever you are on your own in your hermitage or whenever you are in a temple dedicated to Dattatreya, you should not cover your body, except if the weather does not allow it. Our lineage that goes back to Swami Sadashiva Brahmendra Avadhuta, who attained *samadhi* (which means he passed away liberated) around 1752 A.D. in a small village in Tamil Nadu by the Kaveri River, requires that we should always be naked, as remaining unclothed signifies that we do not distinguish between wearing, or not wearing clothes.

'This *samadhi* (place where he passed away), ashram, and temple, are still maintained by the Maharaja of Puddukottai, whose ancestor was an ardent devotee of our *parampara* (lineage) Guru.'

I was listening with great admiration about the successive swamis who also had taken *Sannyas Diksha* after Swami Sadashiva more than 300 years ago and now I understood the hardship they had to face while roaming around naked all over the country. This is what I would have to face soon.

I knew from the reading, discussions, and exercises that my Guruji made me do, that yogis are not only capable of mastering their emotions by breath control, but can also command their body according to their own will-power. This is what one sees in the Himalayas in the winter where many *sadhus* take a bath in the freezing cold gushing streams.

The country is full of stories of yogis who get themselves buried for several days. 'Yogis are capable of slowing down their breath and cardiac rhythm to a point so tenuous, that one could think they are dead!'

My Guru taught me various forms of meditation, but he warned me that meditating is not the be-all and end-all of Spirituality. He recited one *shloka* (verse) of the *Avadhuta Gita* that says —

Why do you meditate shamelessly
when you are the meditator
and the Object of Meditation.

He also taught me humility, to shut my ego and to think and act for others. He instructed me about other spiritual austerity exercises we call *tapasaya*. This Sanskrit word could be translated as 'penitence', as it is called in Christianity. This, however, does not mean self-punishment or self-torture. Not at all! It is in fact a way to make one's resistance leave one's body and mind and master oneself. Not only the body, but also the mind.

I have now been able to develop professional relationships based less on irritability, more on sincerity, and much more on love. I had to bear solitude, worries, and stress without the help of tobacco and alcohol, which of course are very bad for health.

'Everything is only an Illusion,' said my Guruji to me. Hmm, that is very easy to say and not so easy to accept and practise, I thought. I therefore learnt to show anger while not being angry when things were not going the way they should have with our staff. It is necessary to restore some order and discipline amongst the people I deal with in my professional life.

Once the Diksha ceremony was over, Swami Sarveswara told me, 'You will go back to the world, continue to work there because it is there where your talent lies and your work will be of use to everyone. You will be able to help others and share with them what you acquired through Lord Shiva. Even though you will be working in the profession you have been trained for — fashioning garments — you will not be able to wear any of them. You will either be naked, covered by the four winds, as mentioned in many Hindu sacred texts, or clothed with those two pieces of ochre cloth. It should never be ornate or sewn; it should be plain cotton or wool according to the local climate. Another important condition of Sannyas is that you will not sign any contract that will bind you to anything or anyone. You will have to learn how to quieten your thoughts a bit more and let your heart do the talking instead.

'One thought calls for another, which calls for another, which in turn calls for another... it is an endless kind of merry-go-round which in the name of rationality and logic, imprisons us without a window to escape from. Now you will have to be conscious of what you really are.'

18

THE BIRTH OF FASHIONS INTERNATIONAL

The evening of my Sannyas Diksha, I was lying in a 200 square foot room in the ground floor flat belonging to my friend and associate, Jayapalan, in a busy, noisy, polluted area of Madras. He had married in 1987 and we lived there with his young wife, newborn daughter, and his blind father. I used to sleep on a thin mat spread on the floor. No mattress, one thin pillow and a thin bed sheet to cover my body and protect me from mosquitoes that nonetheless, sucked my blood right through the thin cotton sheet. Rats ran over my body and often woke me. Wondering what that was, I would switch on the light and there would be my friend, Mr. Rat, five feet away, looking at me with an amused and taunting look in his eyes. He did not bother to run away. Me neither. We were used to each other. He was a rather cute rat. He seemed to enjoy startling me in the middle of the night.

At five in the morning, I would wake up on hearing the noise of a woman in the neighbourhood who had already begun washing her dishes, even though the sun had not even appeared. The clanging of the aluminium vessels, the rushing sound of the water, the nauseating stench spreading into my room from the open drains outside... this was followed by the sound of her baby crying and her husband shouting, demanding his breakfast.

This was not the end of it yet, as she then continued with her morning chores of doing her laundry, which means relentlessly beating the clothes on a stone. Then her husband would take his bath outside, unmindful of my trying to sleep, while his wife would start cooking his food. There was no way for me to continue sleeping and I just had to get up and do my own morning chores before I could start my daily *sadhana*.

I had decided to sell my knowledge of the garment industry in India to all customers who would like to have their products manufactured here and exported to their countries. Jayapal and I, with another woman who was my personal secretary during the days of Fabratel, created Fashions International in 1988. We had modest beginnings, once again, but thanks to help from my mother, brothers and friends, we could see the light at the end of the tunnel.

We cleared our veranda, which became the office. The constant fumes from the heavy traffic below, floated thick in the air. The blaring horns of cars, lorries, and public buses made conversation impossible. The afternoon sun was constantly on our back till at last, late afternoon, the sun would go down behind the coconut trees on the other side of the street. We had cane furniture only — one table, and two rickety chairs. A typewriter, the kind that are only found in museums today, and a telephone line that I finally managed to get after a four-year wait — that is how one of the most important garment outsourcing offices in India, was born. I was happy to start with a good order from a new customer — Chipie — a renowned French brand based in Carcassonne, with whom we would have a wonderful business relationship for 15 years.

In those days there were no cellular phones, no computers, no Internet as these either did not exist then, or were too expensive for us to afford. If we needed to send a message to a customer, we had to telephone the telegraph department of the Indian Postal Service and dictate the text by reading out one word for every letter in the word: A for apple, B for Bombay, R for Raja, etc. Imagine sending an A4 page of text, it could take me about 15 minutes to dictate the text to the lady who could either not hear properly, or could not understand my French accent. Fax machines did exist, but we couldn't afford our own machine and had to go to the Post Office to receive or send any faxes.

For this we had to travel into the city. We didn't own private transport yet, so the three of us used to pack ourselves into autorickshaws for a bumpy 45-minute drive on badly maintained roads through chaotic traffic. Working through the summers was hard and Jayapal and I had a tough time performing online quality control in the factories with whom we were working. It was so hot that we could not bear it for more than 15 minutes at a time and then we had to go into a room with air-conditioning to keep us alive and refreshed to start another round, until we were satisfied with the quality we were getting from them. It was even difficult to communicate with our customers via telephone as we had to book international calls via operators, which as I explained before, meant an endless wait.

The factories with whom we were working were all located outside the city. It required that we travelled a lot using public transport. We spent endless hours in buses. Autorickshaws were even worse. We were shaken like sacks of potatoes, almost asphyxiating from the pollution, then reached our destination dazed, almost comatose, in a state close to fainting. Our first luxury was to purchase a cycle to go to the nearby Post Office to get our faxes, as we did not own a machine yet. Then, we opted for a small moped, a TVS50 — the cheapest we could find. Even today, you can see many of them in the cities, but more so in the countryside of Tamil Nadu where it is a multipurpose vehicle, used not only for the individual but also as family transport, as they can carry at least four people. It is a kind of multi-purpose lorry as it can precariously carry huge bags of vegetables from nearby markets.

Often, I got stuck with this moped when it decided to go no further. I had to walk miles while pushing it to one of the many repair shops that dot most Indian roads.

My friend Jayapalan and I had to take care of all the responsibilities. I took care of the paperwork, customer relations, and purchases while Jayapal looked after production and quality assurance. At the same time, I had to perform my daily *sadhana* and meditation every morning. In the evenings, alone in my room, I would sit for a while in front of my Shiva Lingam, chant my *japa* (meditative repetition of mantra), contemplate and then read a book on spirituality for a few hours before falling asleep exhausted, not even bothered about my friend Rat's nightly visit.

19

THE ONE WHO HAS AUM IN HIS HEART

This period started to be the most difficult, yet most satisfying time of my life. To be in this Life, but not of it. To be a swami, a monk, while being the steering captain of an enterprise, to renounce all and yet to sign cheques of big amounts, to be naked next to men wrapped up in their suits and ties, or uniforms. What is great in India is that after the initial astonishment when I returned to work after my Sannyas Diksha, my associate Jayapal, my staff, and friends accepted me for what I had become. There was only one exception, our secretary, a Christian woman, who although she called herself my friend, could not come to terms with my new identity. She refused to call me 'Swami' and continued to refer to me as 'Christian'. I did not insist that she stop calling me Christian, and let her call me whatever she wished, after all a name is only a label. I was, however, apprehensive about what my customers would say when I met them during my first trip to France dressed up in such an alien manner. How would our Indian suppliers take it when they saw me as a swami?

At first, I had to adjust myself to this new life and this new way of dressing or rather undressing. I started wearing typical Indian clothing. A kurta (shirt) and pyjamas made from handspun and handwoven cloth in an earthy ochre colour.

Though my Guruji understood why I was dressing up in such a manner, he kept on telling me, 'You must wear *dhoties* soon.'

One day he told me, 'Why do you worry about what others will say? It is your faith. It is your life that you have accepted to live. Chin up and dare!'

The first time I dared to go to France wearing a *dhoti*, I found it to be easier than I thought it would be. I did however hear derogatory remarks such as, 'Are you from the Hare Krishnas?' or, 'Hey Father Christmas, aren't you a bit early this year?'

Until the day when I decided to let the 'dogs bark at the passing caravan'.

Interestingly enough, I never had any problems within our fashion community. Firstly, they would never pass loud comments about the way you dress, since we all take it as a personal statement in the fashion fraternity. People are free to express themselves in the way they feel, expressing their personal sensitivity by the dress they wear.

During business meetings with foreign customers, everyone would at first display surprise, but after a few minutes of 'business talk' their attitude changed as they recognised one of their own tribe by the way I negotiated in a no-nonsense, straight to the point, technically knowledgeable, confident, and inspiring manner.

Of course, business was not always a win-win situation in our line of work and I used to share my disappointments with my Guruji, 'Don't think the life of a Sannyasin is an easy one. People imagine that once you become a monk it is to run away from life. On the contrary, it is a life of responsibilities and commitments and you do not have any excuse for not doing your best.'

I would then forget about feeling low and I would go back to Chennai happier. Am I not Swami Pranavananda Brahmendra Avadhuta, the one who has Aum in his heart...?

20

BEING MONK AND CEO

Incidentally, business truly turned successful the same year that I took Sannyas Diksha and became a Hindu monk. After initial difficulties with Chipie — the buyer in-charge was a tough lady with a very rough way of talking — we started to get good orders. As this brand was very well known in the French market, it was rather easy to get Lee Cooper International, because Chipie's creativity was a kind of guarantee of our way of working. Lee Cooper International, though initially a British brand, was based in Paris. Their top bosses came down to Madras to meet me and visit some of the exporter's factories I wanted to use for production. The meeting went very well, although initially they were surprised to see me in my ochre robes, my knowledge of the industry made a great impact, and we started with a very good order. That was my second customer. In 1989, our breakthrough came when Kenzo was about to become our third customer.

After getting an appointment for this important meeting, I bought a nice camel hair jacket, matching trousers, socks, and shoes to meet them. I could not force myself into getting a tie around my neck and I opted for a manly scarf. I tied up my hair in a ponytail and trimmed my beard, as I did not think a flowing one would create an atmosphere of trust. I had to look 'civilised' and did not want to look like a *paillous* (tramp), or I would not have been able to get past the reception desk. This is how I met the CEO of Kenzo Company. During my meeting I talked to him about India, my work ethics, and, of course, explained to him the great handworked embroidery India has produced for centuries and that all this would be made available to him at a very interesting cost. All those points were important factors that made him decide to try our services. I had learnt what to say and how to say it from my previous meetings with other customers, who would invariably say, 'Oh ! India, never in my life! I had a very big issue when I tried something there years ago.' Or, 'I have a colleague who really burnt his fingers with an Indian factory.' And, 'India? No way, their products are dirty and the quality is horrible.'

I, however, had something else to say.

'Why don't you try me? We will be your office in India. We will do all the following up for you on the shop-floor and we will keep you informed immediately of the progress of your orders and perform a final quality control before they ship the goods to you.'

He liked the idea. He knew that he would be able to increase his company's profit margin substantially. He started the ball rolling with us. After developing samples that met their quality standards, we bagged a big order.

Being financially stronger allowed us to go for a better, more dignified, safer, and more comfortable means of transport. We bought a second-hand Ambassador car.

It was manufactured in the early '60s and was more like a tank, heavy, noisy, polluting, slow, difficult, and dangerous to drive because this vehicle has bad brakes and overturns easily. It is still on sale today and makes up the bulk of airport taxis as well as lower level government official cars. With this car, I drove all over South India from one weaving centre to another, day and night, without a driver. As the steering wheel was a direct drive, I could feel every small pothole and stone. It had no heat insulation between the motor and the passengers, which is why driving in May was hell. The greatest advantage was that one could find a mechanic anywhere in India and even a small boy could repair this vehicle easily. Soon after, we bought a Maruti 800 (Suzuki), the brainchild of Rajiv Gandhi, the leader who opened India to modern times. I had fun with this car, as it was a great improvement from the 'oven on wheels' that my Ambassador was. It had all the latest modern technology, including a functioning air-conditioner — what a luxury! Although it was a 'sardine can' I drove this little toy a lot and by myself.

My already short nights were further shortened by frequent 'power cuts', perennial electricity breakdowns, or planned load-shedding. I remember one night in the scorching month of May, we had one of our dreadful power cuts. No fan, no light, but plenty of mosquitoes that seemed to be the only beings enjoying the power outages. Jayapal, his family, and I, had no choice but to spend a little time in our car, with the engine running and the air conditioning on. Not for long though, as petrol is very expensive in India, or seemingly expensive for us who were far from rich.

Often we had to go to the nearest Electricity Board office to force a team of engineers to come and repair the transformer on the pavement outside our home, from where sparks regularly flew, resulting in regular failures. We had to argue for hours into the night to finally convince the team to give in to this mad foreigner who was always after them and who would not leave them one moment until he got what he wanted — electricity to activate our fans and keep away swarms of hungry mosquitoes from us.

Developing our business with Chipie was an excellent move because this made a good reference to share with our future customers. I remember what the tough lady boss said after getting over her initial surprise of seeing me in my usual Spartan clothing, 'Surely you are well integrated in India and that is what I like.'

We had a long business relationship until 1999, when they sold their brand to another company. I did not continue working with the new management, as I did not agree with their work ethics.

The buyer had been super tough with us and particularly with me, as she was not proficient in English and would vent her frustration to me in French. Most of the time, what irked her was totally unjustified and exacerbated due to some personal issues she had with a very close friend of hers. She had to hit someone... and if there were the smallest issue, she would make a mountain out of a molehill and use filthy words. I remember in the beginning of our business relationship with her, she screamed at me one day on a telephone call from France.

I screamed back at her, minus the filthy words. There was silence at the other end of the line and then she screamed, 'You are mad Christian, go and get treated in a mental hospital!'

'Sure... we should go together then!' I retorted as loudly as I could. Silence on the other end of the line... I hung up.

I thought that was it, I had lost a customer. But, why should I let this person insult us? We are not her slaves. Before this strong altercation, the design team had given me their whole collection to develop in India. I told everyone to stop working on Chipie. One month later, the chief designer called me on the phone from Carcassonne and asked, 'So, Christian, how is our collection progressing? When are you sending us your prototypes for approval? When are you coming back to France?'

'What are you talking about?' I answered. 'Don't you know

how she insulted me over something very silly and she was totally wrong!'

'Come on, Christian... don't take it so badly. She is not a bad woman. She just has a strong character.'

Of course, she was aware of our argument and wanted us to patch up as they all saw a great potential in Fashions International. I did reconcile with her and the next time I went to meet them in Carcassonne, she came to me with outstretched hands, and said with a beaming smile, 'I like guys who have character, who have guts.'

From then on things progressed for the better and our volume of business increased substantially. Word of mouth also worked in our favour and more customers came on their own, to work with us. I can say it was our 'Golden Age' as business boomed. Of course, all this was not without problems. We had tons of them and still do. The three customers we started with grew to 35, most of them in France. Brands also have their peak point and then slowly go down sometimes towards their own death, if they do not act at the right time and rethink their product designs or customer targets.

There is nothing worse than working for many, many years with someone and then finding out that the relationship is over. This happened to a few of the customers we were working with. As I'm writing these lines, I am reminded of Liberto, a brand with whom we worked for 18 years and who had to close down. It had nothing to do with the actual global financial crisis that is shaking all the economies now.

Instead, it was an internal matter, which made their financier pull the plug. Sad, but then that is what Life is all about. Everyone forgets, or rather does not want to remember that Life is also Death.

21

ADVAITA

I do not know much about my Guruji's life (the suffix 'ji' indicates affection and/or respect). Because, in the Hindu tradition, a *shishya* (disciple) never asks his Guru where he comes from, who were his parents, his caste, education, or his achievements. I only know that the lineage we belong to — Parampara Gurus, from where the order name stems, dates back to the time of Sadashiva Brahmendra Avadhuta who lived in the 18th century in the Puddukottai area (near Tiruchirapalli). Sadashiva Brahmendra was his Sannyas Diksha name and Avadhuta was the order he belonged to, based on Advaita as promulgated by Adi Shankaracharya, the Hindu saint reformer of the eighth or ninth century, and from Dattatreya, a quasi-mythical personage who is considered one in the highest state of Advaita. The *Avadhuta Gita*, that he wrote, is considered the highest statement of Advaita. In fact, this text has become my 'Bible' and is always in my bag.

Avadhuta means 'the liberated soul', someone who is devoid of any worldly attachment and who has reached a spiritual state, always aware of the Truth of his Being as the Ultimate. Though the word *Avadhuta* implicates renunciation, it also precludes another state, still higher, which is neither attachment nor detachment, someone who is beyond the traps of duality.

An Avadhuta does not feel the need to follow any rule, whether those rules are secular or religious. He is not looking for anything, does not avoid anything. He does not possess either knowledge or ignorance. Having reached the realisation of the Self intuitively, he lives constantly in a live Consciousness of his realisation. The *Avadhuta Gita* is therefore a Vedantic text that represents the highest philosophy of non-duality in its purest form.

'The Avadhuta, alone and pure, in the equality of his soul, is happy everywhere, even in the most impure place. Having renounced all, he wanders about naked, perceiving the Absolute everywhere, seeing the All inside himself.'

(Chapter I, Shloka 73, *Avadhuta Gita*)

Another verse says —

'He attains the Supreme, the eternal Self, being perfect or not, whether he has full control of himself or not, whether he is in control of his senses or not, whether he is active in Life or not.'

(Chapter II, Shloka 37, *Avadhuta Gita*)

The basis of our thoughts or inspiration is Advaita, one of the greatest philosophical systems of India on which rests the foundation of my Order. One cannot find a more logical, luminous, more complete philosophy than this. Advaita is the doctrine of Non-Duality, which means that there is no difference, no separation between you and the One, that many people call 'God' (in whatever language, by whatever name), or the Ultimate, while some others call Him/She/It/ Truth.

Followers of Advaita prefer to call this 'the Self'. This acceptance of the All is the only way to happiness.

Intellectually, with even a modicum of IQ, anyone can understand what the Self is. It is our true nature, the one that does not change, that is not affected by age, is stable, eternal, and the source for whatever exists, visible, or invisible. In Advaita, the Absolute, which is non-dual, manifests itself in Space and Time. This process brings in the illusion of duality, hence the appearance of shape, the arrival of what we call the 'birth'. However, what birth are we talking about? It is not the birth of the Absolute, which already exists pre-birth, but the birth of the apparent shape of it. For us humans it is all about the apparent shapes, colours, volumes and the Space in-between, entwined with Time and the Energy that keeps it all together, that forms a homogeneous compact, ever-present entity. It is only an impression, an illusion, just like the blades of a propeller engine appear to form a plain disk while rotating at a high speed. The moment the motor stops and the blades stop rotating, the actual propellers appear. The disk has vanished.

It was an illusion since it is not permanent.

Therefore, impermanence is not of interest in our search for what is Real. What is Real has to be permanent and permanence is our Real Nature. The Self.

Spiritual research is therefore the search for the Self. How are we to proceed to achieve the realisation of our Real Self?

Many Masters like Ramana Maharshi, Nisargadatta Maharaj, and Dattatreya, have explained this Realisation of the Self very clearly. To achieve this goal, it is useless to accumulate intellectual knowledge, to be so absolutely adamant to reach at all cost some imaginary level of consciousness that is anyway totally useless. It is enough to eliminate from our heart all that we are Not. Then, as we discriminate, we sort out, to remove what is not necessary, ephemeral, and therefore not Real. We will see that little by little our clinging to this world laden with suffering and illusory joys will disappear slowly and be replaced by an inner peace which can never be disturbed.

Even if anger, despair, or pain shakes your body and your mind, this peace will always come back and take this anger, despair and pain away from you. It is not an easy task. Far from it. It is a work in permanent progress in each instant. Once your intellect has understood this, then it is up to your heart, and that is the hardest part.

It is not necessary, or desirable to stop all physical activities, as you have to find this peace in everything and everyone. Thus, running away from your work, your relationships, and your responsibilities is like running away from your Self. In fact, little by little you will drop the illusion of being the author of actions. It is not simple to do that in the beginning, but with repeated, relentless efforts and with the strong wish to reach the Goal, the Self will bring you victory, as indeed, it is a fight. In short, it is not a question of renouncing one's activities, but rather, to act in such a way that *activities renounce you* and leave you. Work is no more work and actions are no more actions, everything is just a way of being.

In India, people do not so much practise their spirituality as live it, it is part of their day-to-day life, practising yoga and chanting, and singing their *bhajans* while performing their daily *puja* with the whole family around them before starting their day's work. It is for each Indian a very ordinary act, which they do not try to analyse. There is nothing either religious or sectarian about it because for them the material and spiritual life is one, and indivisible.

22

MY GURU AND HIS LINEAGE

We know very little about Sadashiva Brahmendra Avadhuta's life, except a few details. One day as he was resting, lying naked as usual in a field with his head resting on a stone as a pillow, a group of farmers passing by said, 'Look, the *sannyasin* needs a pillow for resting his head!'

Hearing this remark, he took the stone from under his head, threw it away and never used a stone to rest his head on again. Of course, this is only an anecdote, but he is still remembered around Pudhukottai where he walked the forests surrounding the town. People used to throw stones at him while he was begging for his food, but the Maharaja of this town became his most fervent admirer and disciple. He refused to be lodged in the palace and the Maharaja visited him in the forest, seeking knowledge and advice.

Even today, Sadashiva's Samadhi (tomb) is still maintained by the descendants of the Maharaja of Pudhukottai. Before dying, since he knew the day and time of his death, Sadashiva Brahmendra Avadhuta told his disciples, 'On the morning of my death, dig a hole here, once I am in it, cover me with soil and plant a Vilva (Indian sacred tropical tree). Once this is done, a man will come from Benares (Varanasi) carrying a Shiva Lingam to put in front of this tomb, then you must build a temple around it.'

This is how it happened and today, at Nerur, 11 km from Karur, at the foot of Kolli Hills, by the majestic Kavery river, stands his Samadhi with a huge, old Vilva tree overshadowing the Swamiji's tomb and in front of it stands an ancient temple built by the ancestor of the present Maharaja of Pudhukottai.

Swami Sadashiva was the beginning of a long lineage of sages who followed his teachings. The most remembered one is 'Judge Swamigal' (a respectful way of addressing a Swami). Why was he called a 'Judge'?

Simply because he was a judge at the Travancore Court (a princely state in what is now known as Kerala) at the end of the 19th century. During his tenure as a judge, he had to pass a ruling on a murder case. All the evidence was against the accused. The judge felt intuitively that the defendant was innocent, however due to pressure from the British masters he had to inflict on this man the capital punishment. Deeply distressed, he threw his judge's robe away through the window and walked out, never to be seen again in court. He also disappeared from his home, leaving his whole family and friends without any information.

He was seen five years later at Nerur, in Tamil Nadu. He was as naked as Sadashiva Brahmendra and had become an Avadhuta Sannyasin himself. He lived for a long time without many disciples, except for Swayamprakash Brahmendra Avadhuta. The story of how he met his Guru and asked to be allowed to become his disciple is well-known.

The first time Swami Swayamprakash came to meet Judge Swamigal at his hut to ask if he could become his disciple, Judge Swamigal did not answer his question. He did not even bother to look at the young man sitting outside, at the entrance of his hut. Hours passed and from time to time, the young Swami Swayamprakash kept on pleading softly, arms folded in humility as is done in India and yet Judge Swamigal kept mum. Dusk came and darkness arrived. There was no lamp or electricity in the hut. Judge Swamigal did not move or talk and yet the young man kept on humbly repeating his request, which was always met with silence. Morning came and still the young man humbly repeated his request. The answer came in the form of a stone that Judge Swamigal threw at him after shouting, 'Go away!'

He stubbornly remained at the door of the hut and continued to ask to be accepted as a disciple. Seeing the determination in the young Swayamprakash, Judge Swamigal told him, 'Come in and be my *shishya*.'

Swami Swayamprakash Brahmendra Avadhuta became a great sage and his fame spread far outside Tamil Nadu. He had many *shishyas* and my Master was one of them.

Like his own Master, when the time came for his end on December 23, 1958, he was also buried in the Padmasana (cross-legged) position in a bag filled with salt, lowered in the hole dug at a place that had been indicated by him and covered with sacred ashes. A Samadhi was built at this place and a Dattatreya temple was erected above it.

From time to time, my Guruji would say, 'The first time I saw you, I immediately found in you this rare determination for understanding the Spiritual Life.'

Another time he said, 'The apparent fact that you are a Westerner never came to my mind as I see Lord Shiva in you as in everything, everywhere, and every time and not the colour of your skin.'

My Guru told me that he had been a *sannyasin* for many years before I met him for the first time. He had been married like me, but unlike my case, death took his wife away. At that time I thought, after all, is getting divorced not like the death of a part of one's life? But then again, isn't Death the beginning of Birth?

Once I dared to ask him, 'How come you have so few disciples?'

He answered, 'There were lots of men who wanted to be my disciples, but it is not easy for a young man to dissociate himself from the World and yet be in the World. They came and went back to where they came from. However, there is only one I retained, *you*.'

'Why me?' I asked.

'Because it was written and because you too will form great disciples who in turn will become Gurus and will teach the Awareness of the Self.' After some time he added, 'Tell them that Awareness of the Self, the Ultimate, is beyond religions, the Ultimate is Love, pure Love, and nothing more and nothing less.'

I also know that he had a son and a daughter. Unfortunately, they were far removed from the level of Knowledge he had. His son, particularly, was a very bad sort and although I found him a job, he managed to get himself kicked out for theft. He continued with a life of cheating, stealing, and hurting people on his path that led him to suicide.

I do not even know how my Guruji got leprosy. He lost his fingers, then his hands, and then his toes and feet. He was taken to a leprosy dispensary, as there are many in India. Fortunately, the doctors could stop the disease from spreading to his face. Until his last breath, his kind, loving face continued to inspire great peace within me. A few years before leaving us, he suffered from diabetes and had to undergo dialysis every few days. He suffered a lot and the slow poisoning of his body gave us very few precious moments when he was still the kind, loving man I had always admired and loved so much despite the horrible pain he had to go through. Swami Vedananda, who brought me to his Master, passed away in 1999 and my Guru attained Samadhi in February 2005, one month after my sweet mother's death.

I remained the only descendant to perpetuate his teachings and follow the difficult path of Avadhuta.

People came from all over Tamil Nadu, but the people of Ullundurpettai were always with him till his end. He had a kind of prudery about his leprosy-eaten body and covered himself carefully when someone came to visit him. People used to ask him all kinds of questions far removed from spirituality. Some people had lost their goats and asked him where their goats were, or if he could find a good groom for their daughter to marry. He had visitors from all religious backgrounds, not only Hindus, but also Christians, Muslims, and people from all walks of life. Once a Christian policeman came to visit him, as he was accustomed to and after his visit, he told my Master, 'Swamiji, give me your blessings as I have to go to Trichy to meet my future spouse, my family is going to introduce me to her.'

Swamiji answered, 'I will be there too.'

The policeman was taken aback. How could this Swami, without hands or feet travel to Trichy, 150 km away? Over and above that, this man was a Catholic and although he respected him, he was somewhat distrustful of swamis. He dismissed the thought and left. His surprise was great when he got off his bus and saw Swami Sarveswara a few meters away from him. As he approached him, the Swami disappeared as mysteriously as he had appeared.

It was not the first time I heard such a story. I had been told he had some *siddhis* (supernatural powers), powers that come progressively during the course of one's *sadhana* (spiritual practices). Wasn't the multiplication of bread and the resurrection of Lazarus by Jesus Christ, also a form of *siddhi*? Jesus used his *siddhis* because he had a great message to pass on to men and had to persuade the incredulous. If you are open and receptive, there is no need for miracles to convince you. My Guruji told me often that obtaining *siddhis* was not the aim of spiritual life and those Gurus that used them usually regress in their spiritual progress. The real *siddhis* however, are courage, an iron will, and an infallible determination that never weakens.

He very often told me the story of Adi Shankaracharya who went all over India, creating Mutts (monasteries) and often met with brigands, wild animals, and weathered storms, cold and heat, he was a real Siddha. My Guru often said, 'If you ever get some *siddhis* during your *sadhana* never use them for your personal use as they are only by-products of your Tapasaya.'

23

YOU WILL BUILD AN ASHRAM

My Guruji told me, 'You will build an ashram (a community for spiritual upliftment).'

'An ashram? Why? I do not need disciples. You did not build an ashram and you were not looking for disciples.'

It was true that at the age of about 80, Swami Sarveswara had only three disciples in his life. He had roughly pushed some of them away, they did not insist, and ran away, not understanding it was Guruji's way of judging the firmness of their resolution. He gave me a sideways look with his dark eyes that meant he did not want any rebuke from me.

'You will look for a proper place to build it.'

In those days, after visiting my Guruji on the weekend, I would continue my trip for another 250 km as I had found a place where I could practise my spirituality in the midst of pristine greenery. It was a little town called Thiruchengodu, right in the heart of the cotton spinning and weaving centre of India.

This busy little town is built around a big granite hill. There are about 800 steps winding their way up, leading to a big, very ancient temple dedicated to Ardhanareswara (half-Shiva, half-Shakti).

What was more interesting to me was that, at 6 p.m. when the *pujaris* performed the last *puja*, the temple was closed to the public and the whole hill was deserted save for monkeys and other wild animals. Halfway from the temple to the top of the hill, there was a cave, which had been nicely cleaned, it had a cement floor, a door, and a *mandapan* (a kind of marquee open to the wind) with stone pillars and a statue of Lord Ganesh (the son of Shiva who has an elephant's head). This is where I decided to retire to, till I found suitable land for building our ashram. I used to go there on Friday and return by the Monday night bus. Those were real trying times for me. Up there, it was not comfortable at all. No electricity, no water, only nature.

On arrival in that little town, I would buy some biscuits and bananas. Bottled mineral water was not readily available in India at the time. Therefore, I bought many 'cool drinks' before starting to walk uphill. The steps start from the poor area of Thiruchengodu and as I started the ascent, people would come to me and say, 'Swamiji, do not go up now. It is not safe. Too many ghosts there...'

I would answer, 'No problem, those ghosts are my friends. I know how to tackle them.'

I was strong in my resolve. But, the kind people wouldn't let me go up without giving me some food. It was true that the place was rather scary and eerie at night. A few bulbs lit the flight of steps to the temple. After that, it was darkness. When I arrived in front of the temple, all I could see was a lone bulb moving in the strong breeze. I was welcomed by a whirl of plastic bags, the scourge of India, paper and dust flying, with squeaking sounds, and shadows of the sculptures adorning this ancient place.

I used to sit at the entrance of the temple, near the massive, thick, majestic wooden door to catch my breath and cool down. It certainly was a bit cooler. I could hear the noisy town below, the blaring loudspeakers and the cacophony of horns. Up here, silence. No humans. Peace.

Then I would continue my climb to my cave. I thanked Lord Ganesh for allowing me to arrive safely here, and if it was too hot in the cave, I would spread my bedsheet in the *mandapan*, and fold my *dhothis* to use as a pillow and fall asleep.

The first light of dawn, replacing the canopy of stars, usually woke me up gently. Birds were already busy and filled up the silence of the night with their songs. Monkeys were on the lookout for food and I knew that I had to be careful with the little food I had in my bag. Lying on my cloth mat, I would watch them as they tried to come closer and closer to me, wondering what eatables they could take away from me.

Knowing what daring and fiery thieves they are, I had already put my stock of food in the safety of the cave.

It was a trying episode in my spiritual life because since I was a foreigner, a naked swami, I was attracting all sorts of people who would climb those difficult steps just to see me. I had made good friends with the man who was eking out a living selling religious necklaces, ribbons and small images of the Gods, as well as biscuits, bananas, and cool drinks. When the devotees came out of the temple after having taken the *darshan* (blessings) of the deity, he would advise them to go up further and pay a visit to the *Vellakaran* (white-skinned) naked swami, and he would advise them to buy biscuits and bananas to offer me as is the tradition when you visit a swami. They came, bowed to me, touched my feet and placed their offerings at my feet. Out of curiosity, some would ask me questions about myself and others would ask me about their future, as many Indians believe that swamis are capable of predicting the future. Others would ask me what to do about their daughter's marriage as they could not find a suitable groom, etc... I realised that what my Guruji was going through was starting to happen to me.

Following his advice, I let anyone come to me and ask me any question. I would answer them to the best of my abilities, smiling kindly, and let them go back to their home happy. I did, however, refuse to tell them their future.

There were difficult days up there, especially in the summer. The whole hill was a huge block of granite, resembling the famous hill of Rio de Janeiro. The heat would radiate from those huge stones and if there were no wind, it would be unbearable. I made a point not to venture in the sun too much. Sitting cross-legged, meditating, contemplating was peaceful, except for the incessant passage of curious visitors. Often the last breeze would bring a horrible stench from a nearby paper mill, which incessantly belched its nauseating pollution. I had noticed in the distance a darkish mountain range. I asked one of the visitors. 'What is the name of those hills?' Kolli Hills, I was told. I thought that it looked nice and was worth a visit.

24

KOLLI HILLS

In those days, we had a fabric engineer, who was a local, and I asked him about Kolli Hills. He told me, 'Those are beautiful hills, Swamiji. If you wish to visit them, I will take you there.' I jumped at the offer and the next weekend we spent the night in his village home at the foot of Kolli Hills. Early morning, we boarded a small, packed bus and had a scary ride up the hills. We went through 70 hairpin bends. It was a nightmare and many people vomited all the way up to the first stop in Senmedu, the administrative village of Kolli Hills. The highest peak of the hills culminates at 1450 meters and the average height is around 1100 meters. This means it is roughly 8-10 degrees Celsius cooler than the plains below.

This was ideal for me as it was difficult to access, not too many Indian tourists and no foreign ones at all, untouched by modernism with kind tribals inhabiting nearly 230 villages there.

I wanted to find a piece of land and it took me about two years to find the right place. My friend Jayapalan agreed to become the owner of the land I found and we formed a Trust, for running our ashram. I had set four conditions for the land we were looking for.

– It should be away from human habitation

– It should have an access road

– It should have trees

– It should have water

After numerous offers from the broker, one day, I found 17 km from Senmedu, a 3 acre little plot, tucked in between massive hills. It had eucalyptus trees, which I would painfully remove later on, as I was told they were not good for the environment. I said 'painfully', since I do not like to hurt plants and trees. A spring provided sweet water and an electricity line ran across the land. The nearest villages are about three kilometers away on one side and about five kilometers away on the other.

Near the spring was a little temple with a small statue of Lord Ganesh and old clay statues representing some animist gods, and the ancient beliefs of the land. This was ideal for me. I let my friend Jayapalan negotiate the price and the deal was settled. It seemed very cheap to us city dwellers. In fact, much later on, I discovered that we could have bought it for half the price. I like this place very much. Near the top of the pass from one valley to another, as the meandering road starts to go down, I can see the land with its huge eucalyptus trees swaying in the breeze. It was around June and it must have been around 40°C in the plain, but here it was hardly 30°C even at one o'clock in the afternoon.

There was only one path to the spring below, from which we could hear the murmur of its cool water gushing out. It was not a big spring, but considering the month we were in, it was promising for the future. Above our land, was another piece of land owned by a tribal man. His name is Doraiswami. He was watching us and gave us a gesture of welcome. That was when I met him for the first time.

I wanted someone to look after the land, I knew that if we didn't watch it, someone would come and cut the trees. As we tried to make our way through the head-high thorny bushes, Doraiswami's daughter who was next to him, looked frightened of us and when we came close, she ran away screaming. It was the first time she had seen a white man, with a long beard and long white hair. Doraiswami agreed to look after our little land and we offered him a salary for this. As I'm writing this now, he is still working with us and takes care of our vegetable garden, flowers, and temple maintenance, as he is the son of a *pujari*. His daughters are married now, traditionally married at around the age of 15, and have children themselves (who do not cry when they see me).

I tried to get someone to build for me there what I wanted. The plans were drawn up, but I needed someone to give us the correct position of the temple, which I wanted to build first.

For this I contacted a Brahmin (Hindu upper caste, typically well-versed in Hindu scriptures) who was knowledgeable in *Vastu Shashtra*, the scriptures that offer guidance about how to build in the proper manner so that the building will be auspicious. I found a nice man and brought him to our land. He wanted me to build it next to the road.

'Many devotees will come to visit your temple Swamiji.'

I answered, 'I am not building this temple to attract people. I am building it for our disciples who will reside in our ashram. You will build at the other end of the land, far away from the road.'

So now, the entrance is facing east, as per the *Vastu Shashtra*, and our temple is a well-known landmark and devotees regularly come here and pray.

Little by little, our Trust purchased more and more land. For two reasons, the first is to ensure that no one comes and puts up a noisy rice-mill or houses too close to us, thus ensuring our peace is not disturbed by loudspeakers.

The second reason is that we should have enough land to cultivate food and make ourselves self-sufficient. We have planted Arabica coffee and we are proud to have been awarded the 'Best Organic Coffee of India' title in 2008. We also grow pepper here, since the Kolli Hills' pepper is famous for its distinctive flavour. We grow organic vegetables too.

We are very strict about maintaining our ashram — we allow no smoking, no drinking of alcohol, no loud music, no plucking of flowers, no breaking branches, no hunting animals, no killing snakes, or any other creature in our premises, and no throwing plastic and paper anywhere. A bit dictatorial, you may say.

Meanwhile, I had not found anyone who would travel so far, along with his workers, to build what I wanted, to start with at least our temple, two bedrooms, and a kitchen-cum-dining hall. Time went by and there was no one in sight.

Therefore, I had no alternative but to opt for a hut made out of clay and straw with a roof of tiles arranged on beams made from eucalyptus trees. One fine day, Doraiswami and his wife prepared a mixture of soil and water and he built the four walls with a hole for a window on one side and a hole for a door in the opposite wall. We had no actual door or window that could close, except for the hole. We lived in this place, with either the cold winter wind, or our cooking smoke blowing through it, making breathing difficult and our eyes watered endlessly. Winters were hard there. The window only closed with a piece of cardboard, which was not enough to keep scorpions, millipedes, and other insects away. Snakes also had free rein and could find a warm place to hide here. Our greatest fear was cobras. Fortunately, they never entered the hut.

25

LIVING IN A MUD HOUSE

As I planned to get our ashram properly organised, I needed to have a manager who could for the time being stay with me in such minimum comfort. I could not find anyone who would be willing to go through such hardships. One day, as I was arriving from Chennai, I stopped in Senmedu to have my lunch at a restaurant. As I got out of my car, which I was driving alone, a man approached me and spoke to me in good English, 'Good afternoon, Father.'

'I am not a Father, I am a Hindu monk,' I answered.

'May I talk to you for a moment?' he asked.

'Why not? Come with me to this restaurant and we shall talk. Have lunch with me.' The restaurant, the only decent one (sort of) available in Senmedu had been painted some years ago, but the smoke from the kitchen had covered it with black soot, so that we could not make out what colour the paint had been.

Inside there were long wooden tables with benches on either side. Pieces of dirty cloth were strewn on the cemented floor. We sat down and the waiter, whose shirt looked as if it had never been washed since it had been purchased, picked up one of those dirty cloths with his toes and started to 'clean' our table.

We ordered our *thali*, a full South Indian meal comprising white steamed rice and some not-so-spicy vegetable dishes and *sambar*, a vegetable stew, with *dal* (yellow lentils). They served this on a palm leaf, on which the waiter sprinkled some water, the origin of which I did not want to question. Meanwhile, we talked.

He apologised for calling me Father on seeing me, a white-skinned man, he thought, I must be a Christian Father, as he was a Christian from Kerala, the state next to Tamil Nadu. Sunny, that is his name, was in his early twenties and was providing social service to the tribal people of Kolli Hills.

He was mainly helping them get what they were entitled to, because they were unable to write and read and they did not know their rights and entitlements. That is why it was easy for unscrupulous local officials to take advantage of them. Sunny had to walk miles all over our hills to meet villagers and help them, with the meagre income that his uncle was sending him for his desire to help others. He seemed to be a good person.

He was free, unmarried, and offered to help me, and in return I would, of course, take care of all his needs, transport (we got him a second-hand motorbike which he still uses), lodging, and food. We gave him a salary as well as a percentage of the agricultural income we received.

He also had to take care of the tribals living around the ashram, and especially give them some medical help in case of emergency. He accepted my offer and soon joined me and started living in the mud house (without doors or windows). There was no electricity there, or a telephone connection.

We cooked inside the mud house and during the monsoon, with the low clouds covering our ashram, it was damp, cold, and miserable. To take a bath we had to heat up some water from the spring and standing naked in the cold we would take a quick bath and immediately run up to the mud-house to warm ourselves by the fire where our tribal neighbour cooked our breakfast. This went on for a couple of years while Sunny did a lot of work in clearing all the thorn bushes using just his bare hands and his *aruval* (a kind of machete).

One day, Sunny came home with a building contractor from Senmedu who was willing to do the buildings for us. I showed him the plans I had made and we started with the temple first. As the years passed and whenever we had funds available, we built rooms for me and then for visitors, a kitchen and dining hall, and an independent house for Sunny. He got married and has two kids. We gave him a new car so that he could move around safely with his family. Sunny is still with us today, though lately he has experienced difficulties in his personal life. He is not only the manager of our ashram, but is rather like a loving son.

26

WHITE SWAMI WITH THE MATCHBOX CAR

Ten years had passed since Fashions International had set roots, and I could see that everyone was happy, but too cramped in our little office in the busy area of Mylapore in Chennai. We did not have enough chairs for everyone and they often played musical chairs if you were not sitting in your chair for long. Everyone in the company told me, 'Swamiji, please let us find a better place to work.'

Hence, Jaypalan and I started to hunt around for a suitable place which was not too expensive, but we only came upon places, which were not suitable, or were too far away etc. Finally, one exporter with whom we were working, told us he wanted to sell a portion of his land. We visited it and found it ideal for our business, a quiet, clean area in a decent neighbourhood. Fifteen minutes from the airport, and five minutes from a five-star hotel. Great. We swiftly purchased the land.

We called a lady architect and commissioned a design that should not only match my requirements, but also be functional, full of natural light, with nature inside the office. It should be ultra-modern, and yet traditionally South Indian. A blend of East and West with a tropical jungle in the centre surrounded by glass so that my staff could see the rain falling on the frangipani trees while working.

The whole office has Internet connectivity through Wi-Fi, the latest computer technology, and is fully air-conditioned. One of our customers, when he visited our office the first time joked, 'Where is my room? And the swimming pool?'

I am often asked if the fact that I am a Shivaite monk is a handicap for our business in France. Today, all my customers know me as 'Swami' and I do not really worry about this. What is important is the confidence they have in our capacity for 'delivering the goods', if I can perform correctly and if they get value for the money they pay us.

When I was still driving myself, the tribals of Kolli Hills had given me the name *Matchpetti Vandi Vellakaran Swami* (the white swami with the matchbox car) and often I had to drive in the worst possible conditions. It really felt like I was driving a matchbox. One night during one of those difficult trips, with a *shishya* accompanying me, at around one o'clock at night, we began experiencing a terrible storm and the road was like a furious stream of water.

I couldn't see the edge of the road, my left wheels went off the road and I heard a metallic sound as the bottom of the car scraped against the road. I swerved towards the right and was able to regain stability. We continued onwards, trying to avoid the road edge and fallen trees. Then came the start of the 70 hairpin bends. Huge boulders had rolled down the hill and were blocking half of the road. Thanks to the size of my car, I could make it through and finally reached a height where we found ourselves above the clouds. Even then heavy raindrops battered our small car. Adamantly, we continued until we reached our ashram where Sunny was waiting with umbrellas. This nightmare trip had lasted 15 hours instead of the usual nine hours. We were exhausted, but happy to have reached our destination safely.

Sunny had married a Protestant girl from Bangalore, both of them hold a Bachelor Degree in Theology. Sunny is a Syriak Christian. They are the direct descendants of the Indian Brahmin Caste of Kerala who had been converted to Christianity by Saint Thomas who came from Palestine and reached the shores of Kerala in the first century AD. Saint Thomas had continued eastward and stayed in Madras for the rest of his life. Today, one can still see the relics of St. Thomas in the beautiful St. Thomas Cathedral in modern day Chennai. We can say that the Christians of Kerala are the earliest Christians of India and certainly earlier than those in France.

Ruby is a lively woman who has been very willing to help us in our objective of bringing hygiene awareness to the surrounding villages, especially to women and children. With the help of chemist friends in my French hometown, I collected surplus medicine, which was still fit for consumption, and brought them to our ashram. Of course, we couldn't cure serious diseases, in case someone fell very ill they were taken down to a hospital in Namakkal, a small town at the foothills.

Our little dispensary was helpful for those suffering from headache, toothache, colds, indigestions, cuts, burns, skin rashes, etc. and even venereal diseases. They could also stitch up deep wounds after I brought the equipment from France.

It was incredible to see people walk to our ashram from afar to get solace and free treatment from us. Unfortunately, the French government banned the distribution of the medicine, so now we are left with only disinfectants and painkillers that we buy from Chennai, and other nearby towns. Our tribal friends were so thankful for the free services that Sunny and Ruby provided, that they often came back with a bag full of rice, or vegetables for us. Our role, specifically, is to give women some health care education that will help them have healthier children, by being healthier themselves. Women in this part of South India take a bath once a month and the same is the case with the children. Many women and children are often covered with skin rashes and have sexually transmitted diseases, because the men and women are promiscuous by nature.

The nearby town of Namakkal is infamous for having the highest incidence of AIDS in India, spread by the truck drivers who visit the city for carrying out the maintenance and body-building of their trucks, which is the thriving industry of this town. Therefore, we had to treat women who came to talk to us about their vaginal problems and we had to call their husbands also. I could easily understand what the problem was, as they looked shy and murmured their problems only to Sunny or Ruby. Unfortunately, we could not test whether they were positive for HIV AIDS, but we could at least treat the common venereal diseases.

I was getting more and more worried about the way traffic was getting heavier in the town and the roads were not being maintained or upgraded. Add to this the fanatical way in which most locals drive which is downright dangerous and egoistic. Their motto is often cited as, '*Ien road, ien vandi, poya* (This is my road, this is my car, get out of my way)!'

I suffer heavily because of this attitude. One night at around 9.30 p.m., I was still about 130 km from our ashram, I had left Chennai at around 2 p.m. So far, I had managed to get past the deadly traffic of ruthless bus drivers carrying their overload of travellers. I was alone in the car and going at a steady 80 km per hour when suddenly I was blinded by a bus coming from the opposite direction. The driver was playing with his lights as all drivers do. In a split second, I saw a cart drawn by two bullocks with the driver happily sleeping on top of a huge pile of rice bags, as the bullocks knew the way. This is a common sight on rural roads. I had no choice but to hit the bullock cart.

The alternative was the bus coming towards me at high speed. I applied the brakes hard and braced my body against the steering wheel. I heard the tyres screech loudly. The bonnet hit the back of the cart, and bags of rice flew in all directions. The cart driver, who woke up with the heavy jolt, flew above the bullocks and landed on the grass on the side of the road. He staggered up and looked around dazed. One of the bullocks was dead. The bonnet of my 'sardine can' was pushed into the car, ending a few centimetres from my eyes. Thank God there was no one sitting next to me, or they would have died. I was equally dazed, I did not know what to do in this seemingly remote place, where people had started to appear from nowhere out of the darkness.

Soon, we were surrounded. The cart owner wanted to beat me up, understandably forgetting the significance of my robes. Luckily, a police car passed by and saved me from the angry villagers. We settled the matter by giving the cart owner enough money to buy another bullock. The cart was not damaged, save for one of the wheels that needed to be straightened. My car however was badly damaged and there was no way I could continue home.

I called Jayapal from the nearby village, these were the days before cellular phones. He contacted our friend in Salem, 70 km from the place of the accident. He came, spoke to the local authorities and the owner of the cart, and brought me to our ashram.

The whole of Fashions International came to visit me, as they were all worried about my health. I decided that in order to stay alive on this planet, I should have a safe vehicle to travel to and from our ashram. With the economy of this country improving rapidly, people are bound to own more and more cars, lorries, buses, and considering their horrible civic sense, the roads are being transformed into war zones. If you were to travel on Indian roads, you would see them dotted with mangled wrecks of buses, lorries, and cars. Since my last accident, I do not drive long distances alone and never at night, except going up into the Kolli Hills itself, since at night we can see the headlights of lorries and buses hurtling down the Hills.

We now have a Ford four-wheel drive SUV that allows me to drive comfortably with limited risks. Going up or down the Hills, I do not allow my driver to pilot me as he scares me with his maddening ways, so when we get to the foot of the Hills, I tell him, 'Now it is my turn to scare you. I will drive and you sit next to me.'

Actually, I like driving and it is one of the pleasures I feel I should enjoy.

27

THE PINK STRAWBERRY IN THE FOREST

'You have to deliver a message to the West,' Swami Sarveswara told me one morning and he repeated what he told me when we first met, 'One day you will be known all over the world.'

I was very surprised when I heard this. Nothing was further from my mind than the idea that one day, a journalist would write an article about me, which would be published in a leading French magazine. This article would trigger a series of interviews on all the French TV channels, articles in French magazines, leading newspapers and a book as well. Recently, Discovery Channel and CNN visited our facility. The Indian media came too.

It started with a Tamil investigative magazine called *Junior Viketan* (roughly translated as Junior, with double-meaning talk). Two young men came to meet me at the hermitage on a cold day in the Kolli Hills. They did not tell me they were journalists. As most visitors to the hermitage, they wanted only advice, which I readily gave them.

At the end of the conversation, they asked if I would mind if they took a picture with me. I allowed them to take a picture. Three days later, when I arrived in our office, my friend asked me, 'Did you give an interview to journalists at the hermitage?'

I was astonished and said that I had not.

'You are all over Tamil Nadu on the front page with a banner across your private parts that read — 'The swami who is afraid of people'.' They showed me a copy of the magazine, which is read by almost every household in Tamil Nadu, which has a population as big as France. The 'investigative reporters' had described me as a German swami. They said that I 'looked like a pink strawberry in the forest'. Even though it was full of incorrect information, it was a nice article. Many more Indian magazines came to visit me after this one. I am used to them now, but I make sure that they do not distort the truth of what I tell them.

When my Master fell ill due to diabetes, he stopped eating, lost weight, and experienced dizziness. Without telling us what he needed, he called a Muslim doctor to see him, who told him he had some form of cancer and had only a few months left to live.

I got a phone call in Madras from the woman who looked after him in my absence.

'Swamiji has had his head shaven. He has completely stopped eating and has decided to let himself die.'

I rushed to Ullundurpettai, 200 km from Madras.

'After all, dying from cancer is a honourable death. Ramana Maharshi and Ramakrishna Paramahamsa also had the same disease.'

For once, I forgot about the traditional respect I had to show my Guruji and I talked to him in a harsh and commanding manner, 'Maybe you are not interested in your body. We, however, do care for it, as for us, your disciples, your life is much more precious.'

An Indian disciple would never have dared to say such words. To raise one's voice against one's Guru is considered sacrilege. I had him taken almost forcefully in a car and had him driven straight to one of the best clinics in Madras. There, after many tests it was discovered he had tuberculosis, which was very common in India. We had him start treatment and he was cured. He started eating again and was his usual self till diabetes, a side-effect of the anti-leprosy treatment he had to take continuously, finally took him away from us.

I often asked him to come and stay in our Kolli Hills hermitage, as I would have looked after him and assured him of a comfortable, clean, and peaceful life. He never said no. Actually, a real Guru never says 'no'.

'Come Guruji, to our hermitage…'

'Yes, yes, maybe one of these days.'

I knew that he would never come.

I am frequently asked whether I am the next Guru of the Avadhuta lineage. It is true that today I am the main disciple of Swami Sarveswara, his previous *shishya* married recently. The only picture one sees in his small ashram is one of him and me together. He often made me understand that I am his only and main disciple.

'You should go all over the World and explain what Lord Shiva is, and what Hindu Spirituality is,' he would say.

After an article about me appeared in *Le Point*, one of the most important magazines in France, I was inundated with requests to appear on all the major TV channels in France. Once back in his humble ashram, I showed him a cassette of the TF1 TV (France) programme on which I had appeared, and he was very happy and joked, 'You are now a television star?'

That a Westerner could become the Guru of the great lineage of Advaita Vedanta could seem strange, but why not? We live in the 21st century and all racial and religious barriers have to be abolished. Many priests, nuns, and even Indian bishops from Kerala and Tamil Nadu have gone to Europe. Then why not a French Hindu monk?

This is also the result of the extraordinary tolerance of India. This country accepts the concept that God can manifest Himself in different manners and ways. Today, one of the most important political parties of India is led by an Italian and Catholic lady, Mrs Sonia Gandhi.

FROM MY ALBUM

As a toddler at age two

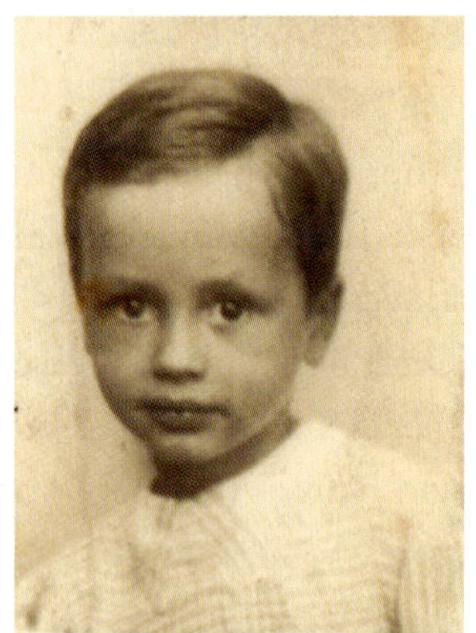

As a kid

In my teens

As a young Swami

With my siblings

My family—
Mom, Dad, sister Annie
& younger brother Gerard

Military service

Just Married

At a beach with my son

In Paris, at an IBM convention

With Mom in France

In Chennai 1972, Greenways Road, with wife, son, mother-in-law and caretakers

Whiling away time after my divorce

Having a gala time with my brothers
Jacques & Gerard (now no more)

Initial days with Jayapalan

With Mom at our factory & with employees in Chennai

Raji,
my initiator to Spirituality

Before I took Sanyas

With Geethanjali—Jayapalan & Chithra's Daughter

With my Guruji Swami Sarveshwara

28

MY GOOD-LIFE LOVING FAMILY

My family was great and accepted what I had become, even though my mother discreetly vented her resentment.

'You look like a *paillous*.' Every time I returned home from India, she would tell me the same thing, and indeed, I understood her feelings, I did not fit into the French environment.

When I arrived at our home in Beziers, she would invariably say, 'You can be a Buddhist or a Hindu, or whatever you want to be, but you should dress correctly. What about your customers, what are they going to think and say when they see you attired in such garb?'

'Let him live his life the way he wants,' my younger brother Gerard would answer and we would all laugh.

Like many other families, we had our share of tragedies. My father died when he was 53, of a heart attack, and our mother had to work hard to educate my younger brother Gerard, and my sister Annie. Later on and not so long ago, both my brothers, Jacques and Gerard, died of lung cancer. They were heavy smokers, like I had been. My young nephew followed them to the tomb and my mother gave up life after a long struggle with Alzheimer's disease.

Even though I am a Hindu monk and know that the World is an illusion and this body will go, I still experience human emotions exactly like everybody else and I don't try to deny it, as I strongly feel this is precisely what makes us human.

Living in India, I had the good Karma to have met my Guruji who made me look at Life as only a transient stage, to enjoy the moments one is passing through, as it will not come back. That is what I have been taught.

Yoga, *pranayama* (breathing exercises), meditation, and contemplation have indeed been useful when facing these hardships. In our family, we loved the good life, we enjoyed good food and drink (without getting drunk), fine wine, and *pastis* (anise-based drink from the south of France), shared with friends. I saw both my brothers become skeleton-like (weighing hardly 35 kg), lose all their hair, and even their moustaches were eaten up by chemotherapy. I had to carry my elder brother to his bed in the hospital in Paris where he breathed his last. Lying in bed, he spoke his last words to me, 'Go now. Go home and look after *Maman* (mother). I am much better.' I hesitated. He insisted that I should go back to Beziers and look after our Mom.

I tucked him in and left. I could not find anyone in the hospital to tell me what his situation really was. I did feel however, that he would not stay with us for long. I took the train to Beziers. Once there, early in the morning, I got a phone call from my sister-in-law in Paris.

'Your brother has left us.'

I turned around and looked at my mother. She understood what had happened and said, 'Why him? Why not me, I am too old.'

We drove back to Paris immediately with Mom crying softly next to me.

Looking at my brother Jacques lying in the hospital bed, so emaciated, so vulnerable, I realised how ephemeral life is. This man was in good health a year ago, enjoying every moment of his life and working hard. When he was younger, he was a gymnast. What is the need of thrashing oneself around? He was only 52 years old. He did not even have time to enjoy the house he was building for himself in a village not far from the Mediterranean Sea where he could fish and be closer to our younger brother.

Then I really understood the Indian Scripture *shlokas* (Sanskrit verses), 'Oh, ignorant, why do you run after pleasures when you are soon going to die?'

Then it was the turn of Gerard, who is seven years younger than me, and is married to an adorable woman and has a son. Another one who enjoyed life, like my elder brother

Jacques, he enjoyed eating well, smoked heavily, and drank just as much. He was an excellent cook and often invited his friends home. He was a generous man and *pastis* always flowed freely at his home, especially when policemen came home. He had a working relationship with the police, since he was the civil servant in charge of revoking drivers' licenses for over-speeding.

At the age of 45, the first warning signal was his cardiac problem. A known scenario was again starting to unfold. 'Lung cancer,' the doctor told him, 'you have one year to live.' He called me the next day, I was in India.

'Christian, I am going to die.'

I tried to talk to him, to bring some peace to his heart... but can one talk of spirituality when someone is dying?

No. The only thing I could think of was to show him all my love by being near him, whether I was in India, or France. He loved cars and I bought him a good and powerful one. He loved it and was proud of it. I also invited him to India, as he had never been here. Actually, the farthest he had travelled outside his own country until that time was Barcelona, 260 km from Beziers. One day I told him, 'Why don't you and Arlette come to India?'

Silence.

'I am sending you two business class tickets.'

One week later, he and his wife landed in Madras. I asked the whole of Fashions International to take care of them, help them discover the city and make him feel that he was not alone in this world. Every one of them was hospitable, as only Indians can be.

My younger brother seemed to live again. He laughed, admired the country, and discovered its many remarkable cultures which change from state to state, and its landscapes — from the coconut palm trees that fringe the romantic beaches of Kerala and its backwaters that we explored on a boathouse, to the Palace of Mysore, the majestic temple of Madurai, the simplicity and the genuine affection of rural South India. Suddenly he discovered the world and that its borders do not stop at Marseille and Barcelona. India had touched him, the way she touches most visitors.

Gerard had caught the travelling bug. He had an urge to see as much of the world as he could. I invited him for a second trip to India. He could feel that he was nearing his end.

He accepted this fate and returned. The second time he looked more tired, frail, and he felt cold in a normally air-conditioned room. This time I took them to North India, the Taj Mahal, Rajasthan, and its palaces.

We lodged in the Jaipur Maharaja Palace. We drove up to Joshimath in the heart of the Himalayas where he admired the majestic snow covered Nanda Devi. We went to Benares (Varanasi) to admire and feel the holy presence of Lord Shiva. It was the last city he visited before returning to France. As he was about to board his plane in Benares, he told me, 'See, I do not think I have much time left for me. Please take care of Arlette and mainly of *Maman*...'

After dropping them off at the airport, I shifted quarters from the magnificent five-star Taj Hotel where I lodged with them, to an 'All Stars Hotel' with a direct view of the burning ghats. My room was on the top floor and opened onto a big common veranda, shared with the next-door room. My bedroom roof was made of corrugated iron sheets on which monkeys jumped all day long. They startled me awake every morning.

The partition between my room and the neighbour's, was made of irregular planks, leaving big gaps at places, through which I not only could see what was happening on the other side, and vice versa, but also got whiffs of the *ganja* my neighbours were smoking almost always.

The neighbours had also noticed me and were wondering who the European sadhu on the other side of the disjointed plank partition was. One morning, as I was taking my bath on the terrace, a tall, skinny, white, blond young man walked towards me. He walked unsteadily, as if he was drunk. After a few moments, we started talking and got acquainted. He wanted to know who I was, what I was doing there, why I had become a Swami, etc. He also told me his story. Claus had a difficult relationship with his father, who found escape from his predicament by spending six months in Varanasi where *ganja* was easy to get and he lived cheaply by spending money his loving grandmother was sending him regularly.

Just before his six-month visa expired, he would take the bus, drive to nearby Nepal, and get a further six months' extension to his visa. Back in Varanasi, he would continue his routine of *ganja* smoking and *bhang* drinking (a mixture of curd, *ganja*, and other 'herbs'). From time to time, he would eat some *chapattis* and *dal* in a non-descript footpath eat-out.

Claus invited me for lunch and took me to his usual hangout, somewhere in a narrow, stinky, crowded by-lane of Varanasi where Madrasi (from Madras) food was available. I enjoyed the *masala dosais* while he preferred his dose of *bhang*. He was a bit disappointed that I refused to drink it or smoke his enormous *ganja* cigars, which he would roll constantly.

He was fascinated by me and wanted to know more about spirituality. The *sadhus* sitting on the *ghats* along the Ganges are on the lookout for young Westerners looking for a fix of *ganja*, because they can extract money from them, while rarely talking to them about spirituality.

Most of the time they do not know anything about Hindu spirituality themselves, as those sadhus are either self-made, or illiterate men, trying to escape their hard life as householders, or trying to evade the police who are after them for some mischief. They get easy money from gullible Hindus and the foreigners thronging the *ghats* and temples of Varanasi. Those sadhus don't know much about spirituality and have nothing to offer foreigners in terms of Knowledge, not to mention being able to explain the mysteries to a devout. All they do is talk about vague rituals, and hum unintelligible so-called mantras. Thanks to me, Claus had a Frenchman, fresh from his ordainment as a swami, educated in Western and Cartesian logic, that would enable him come closer to spirituality and understand the whys of his Being.

When our meal was finished and his second glass of *bhang* was gulped down, we went back to our hotel where again he made himself another huge cigar of *ganja*, while talking ceaselessly.

After a while, he simply collapsed on his bed, fully asleep, to wake up only late in the afternoon the next day. When he woke up, Claus emerged from his smoky bedroom onto the rooftop veranda with stoned eyes and unkempt hair. I told him, 'Come, let's go out.'

I took him out for a strong coffee and said, 'How long will you continue to live this useless way? One year? Two years? Look at that European guy,' I said, pointing to another young man far away, thin as a skeleton wearing dirty clothes, walking with difficulty, aimlessly, and looking completely high. 'Do you want to end up like him?' I asked.

This question woke him up completely.

I took him to our hermitage. From the moment of our arrival, he completely stopped taking *ganja* (anyway it is not available there). He stopped smoking and he performed his *seva* quietly without complaining. Meditating in our temple helped him face the smoking addiction and its withdrawal symptoms.

One month later, he returned to Germany, fresh, and with a strong determination to live in peace with his father. He started studying again. After obtaining a Masters degree, Claus is working with a very important UN agency helping the development of people and nations. He married a charming lady and comes to visit us regularly in our hermitage. I must say I am very happy with his achievements.

29

MAHA KUMBH-MELA

The Maha Kumbh Mela is the greatest pilgrimage on Earth. Maha Kumbh Mela, also known as the Great Kumbh Mela, is conducted every three years in one of four distinct locations, namely Allahabad (Prayag), Haridwar, Ujjain, and Nashik where, according to the *Puranas*, the mythical drop of *Amrith* (Nectar of Immortality) dropped out of a *Khumb* (pot) carried by Garuda. During the three months, nearly 20-30 million Hindus of all sects and all castes gather on the banks of a sacred river, like the Ganga, depending on the location of the city, in order to get the benefit of that Immortality Nectar. The date of this colossal happening is decided by various heads of important Mutts or Hindu religious institutions, according to the position of the moon and other planets.

I had read many articles and books about this incredible

gathering of people and I felt it was paramount for me to attend. I sort of felt pushed towards it.

In 1998, the Maha Kumbh Mela took place in Haridwar, situated at the foot of the Himalayas on the banks of the Ganga. I had visited this place earlier and it held a great attraction for me. I decided to participate along with Sunny, Ani, and Claus.

Ani, Sunny, and I met Claus in Haridwar. I had decided to participate in this Kumbh Mela because I had heard about this amazing gathering of people and its importance for every Hindu in the world, and more particularly, for Naga Sadhus (naked sadhus). I needed acceptance into one of their Akhadas, a sort of association, some of which had been created in the 8th century AD. The Akhadas are headed by Mahants. Each Akhada is given its due place in the various ceremonies during the Kumbh Melas according to their date of creation. Would they accept a white man, a Frenchman, amongst themselves?

One month earlier, I had my secretary Pinky, who speaks fluent Hindi, contact the person in question to introduce me to the highest Akhada, the Juna Akada. She got in touch with the relevant persons at the right places and we found ourselves completely taken care of by devoted Hindus of the Tourism Department in Haridwar. One of them went around the town asking Akhadas if they could accept a small group of South Indians, led by a French white naked swami. All but one refused. The Juna Akhada accepted us after I showed them pictures of my Guruji and told them about the

Parampara Guru lineage. In fact, there is little connection between various Hindu organisations from the south and the north. I was told that North India has a Swami culture, whereas the South has a Temple culture.

This can be witnessed in the superb, majestic, imposing temples of the south as opposed to the relatively smaller ones of the north. While people from the north have a very strong reverence for swamis and consult them regularly when in trouble, this is not so common in the south, except perhaps in the countryside. Finally, I was a member of the Juna Akhada and was allowed to set our tent on the banks of the Ganga.

We reached the sadhus' quarters, a city of tents, some richly decorated with colourful festoons and flags. It really looked like a fair with each tent selling its products. Loudspeakers from each tent were calling for 'customer' devotees. It was an incredible cacophony and a riot of colour in a mass of humanity and a haze of smoke. Outside every sadhu's tent, the *dhuny* (sacred fire) was kept burning until they left the camp at the end of the Mela. The smoke mixed with the smell of *ganja*. We rented a tent for the four of us and pitched it on the little space left for us to use.

We were approaching the day the Kumbh Mela officially began and buses coming from all over India belched out batches of colourfully dressed people. The dark people from the south, the men from Rajasthan dressed in white, wearing magnificent bright turbans, and their women who covered their face with veils. A little India was assembling here.

We made our *dhuny* and prepared our dinner. Before going to sleep, we decided to take a tour of our area. Big and small tents lined both sides of a road, which was filled with a multitude of people belonging to various Hindu denominations. Some followed Lord Shiva, some followed Lord Vishnu, and some others followed Shakti. Akhadas that didn't have their headquarters in the main city's ancestral buildings, had pitched their tent in our area and scores of naked *ganja*-smoking sadhus were assembling there. Some were surrounded by their little courts of devotees comprising Indian men and women, besides many 'hippy' looking foreigners. All sadhus were covered with ash (as I would be the following day). Some were either in meditation or practising severe *tapas* (penance), such as standing on one leg for years without sitting, others had one arm raised for years, to the point where the nails had overgrown and curled up, and the muscles had atrophied.

Another sadhu had his penis rolled around a stick and others had tied heavy stones to their penis to sublimate their sexual powers. Ani, Sunny, and Claus, who were not naked like me, were in awe of what they saw around them. Their eyes popped out in astonishment.

What a show for the end of the 20th century! More than a 1,50,000 naked sadhus had converged here from their ashrams, caves, and hideouts from all over India. Many from the Himalayas, where they remain through the year, living naked in caves surrounded by glaciers.

An incredible noise pervades the whole area. In each

Akhada, each important tent belonging to a known, or unknown swami, or Mahant (head of a group of sadhus) would be packed with crowds howling and screaming their religious chants the entire day and night. They seemed to be competing with their neighbours to see who could be the loudest. This would continue till three o'clock in the morning where there would be a little respite of an hour, and then it would pick up momentum and volume from four o'clock onwards to a point where it would be difficult to have a quiet conversation.

In the evening, each tent is busy cooking dinner, according to the wealth the sadhu has. Modest and poor sadhus will eat a simple dish of *dal* (lentils) and a few chapattis cooked on their *dhuny* by the young sadhus as part of their *seva* (selfless work), while the older ones smoke their *chillums* of *ganja* that is passed around. The air is so full of *ganja* smoke that one gets high just by strolling around the area.

Of course, some sadhus are obviously canvassing for new devotees/disciples, while others are just smoking *ganja* all day long instead of meditating and are in a perpetual state of floating. Originally, the sadhus who lived in the Himalaya used *hashish* to not feel the cold. Nevertheless, one feels that all the people here are moved by the search for God, the feeling of the 'Invisible', of what is above our ego and ordinary mind. There are also many foreign visitors in this huge assembly of people, some have come with the curiousity of a tourist, some because they have heard that sadhus possess *siddhis*, supernatural powers, others are really following a spiritual quest and also some are here for a free *ganja chillum.* One can see sadhus surrounded by foreign 'seekers', passing a *chillum* from one to the other while chanting 'Om Narayanan' (another name for the Ultimate), each time they inhale the smoke. Despite our refusing offers to smoke *ganja*, we were a bit high just by being passive smokers. I, of course, never smoke as I feel there is no need to smoke to reach the Consciousness of the Ultimate.

We had pitched our tent in such a way that the entrance was reserved for people to visit me, and there were plenty of them, as they were attracted by the fact that I am white.

The end of one corner was devoted to my spiritual practice where I had installed the picture of my Guruji and Lord Shiva. Another corner housed our cooking implements and food. At night, we slept like sardines in a can. At about 5 a.m., we were woken with a jolt by a resounding call — 'DHOODH, DHOODH!' (Milk) as the milkman passed by and stuck his head inside our tent. He asked for a bottle, and filled it up with milk for the day.

This time of the day was also when everyone there would wake up and want to answer the call of Mother Nature. This is the time of day when the entire marquee scatters and squats in the meadows along the banks of the Ganges, to relieve themselves. The notion of hygiene is however, not forgotten here. There is a meadow for men and another for women to squat. The organisers sent several teams of two people each, carrying a huge rattan basket with big handles and a shovel with which they picked up people's excretion. They would then sprinkle disinfectant over the area.

Once our daily morning routine was over, we would go to the Ganga and take our bath, not only to clean our physical body, but also to wash away our Karma, as is believed by devoted Hindus. Others performed their daily *puja*, to invoke the Mother Ganga. They made little boats out of fresh big leaves, placed some flowers in it, along with a wick and a little clay oil lamp as offerings to the sacred river.

Here, the river was always carrying small floating leaves that carried in it flowers and a little flame that jumped up and down with the waves of the cool Ganga waters.

This divine river rushes down the Himalayas from Goumukh (Gangotri) from a height of more than 4000 metres, some 250 km away from here. The water is very cold, as it gushes downhill and then spreads into the plains once it reaches the foot of the mountains. The current is so strong that one has to be very careful when dipping into the waters. Doing so thrice in the freezing cold holy water is an achievement. Then it's time for *sadhana*.

Meditating when it is so cold early in the morning, with a thick fog spreading over the city of tents, and the loudspeakers blaring away, is indeed difficult. Next, it is time for breakfast. Ani would start the *dhuny*. He gave us succulent meals of chapattis with *sambar* and a steaming cup of coffee. Later on, there would be a string of visitors, who wanted to ask me questions. Amongst the visitors, were a few who were just curious to meet a white Naga Swami (naked swami), but a lot of Indians came to find solutions to their problems.

A rumour had spread about us. People speculated about the white Naga Swami smeared with ashes, wearing Rudraksha *malas* the South Indian way, and more importantly, who was not smoking anything. My little group comprising Ani, Sunny, and Claus had also been noticed as much for their kindness as for the fact that a white blue-eyed German was part of this group.

Some people asked me practical questions, to which I was trying to give as good an answer as I could, and as far as I could understand their needs. The majority spoke only Hindi and this made our conversation difficult. Ani and Sunny know bits and pieces of Hindi and we could manage to converse with people, with a lot of misunderstanding and heaps of fun. Some people would just sit in front of me for hours, without taking their eyes off me. I must say that I felt embarrassed by those visitors and did not know what countenance to keep. All of a sudden, after one or two hours of looking at me, they would prostrate themselves, touch my feet, stand up and with folded hands, they would respectfully say 'Namaste', and rush away as though they just remembered an appointment they had somewhere else. As usual, they would leave me some money as an offering, as custom dictates. Fortunately, our company provides me with what I need to live a simple life and I did not need more than that. We never asked anyone for any donation and whatever was given to me by those devotees would never have been sufficient anyway.

I do not like to beg for my upkeep and have always preferred to work for it. In general, sadhus at the Kumbh Mela have no qualms about asking for money from passing pilgrims who are constantly reminded that they must be generous. Not so long ago, it was honourable to be a swami. If one saw a saintly looking person sitting silently and meditating, with eyes closed, passers-by would quietly keep some money next to him. Nowadays, however, there is too much poverty in India and there are so many fake swamis that people are wary of them.

I thoroughly enjoyed being at the Kumbh Mela though it was far from being comfortable. One night it rained so much that water dripped through the canvas of our old patched tent. A strong cold wind shook the tent and the four of us had to collect our bedding and huddle together below the peak of the tent.

We were totally drenched and our teeth chattered inspite of all our endeavours to keep warm. Soon, our friend from the Uttar Pradesh Tourism Development Agency who had helped us gain admission into the Juna Akhada, stuck his head into the entrance of our tent and said that he had brought a plastic sheet to put over our tent. We were touched by this mark of friendship and devotion. Ani and Sunny immediately covered our tent and the water dripping through the canvas ceased. Our friend had also brought us a gas cylinder and a stove.

We immediately prepared a very welcome cup of hot coffee. The tent dried after some time and it got warmer inside, while it was still pouring outside. We had to continue to keep watch for any holes through which water could leak. The rain stopped as suddenly as it had started, but then the wind picked up and we had quite a job to ensure our tent didn't fly off...what an adventure!

The food we cooked was wholesome and more than enough. Plenty of rice — a South Indian man cannot live without his daily dose of rice at each one of his three meals — hot sambar with vegetables and some chapattis too. Drinking anything there was a problem as Claus and I had the fragile digestive systems of Westerners and running in the middle of the night with a pail of water to the meadows in total darkness, cannot be called a moment of relief. We were saved yet again by our friend who brought us the plastic sheet during the downpour. He came one morning with a crate of mineral water and though we insisted on paying for it, he didn't take it.

The rain had stopped and the cacophony by the Ganga picked up louder than ever in the crisp cold night. It became so loud that despite the earplugs I had collected from the airlines during my numerous voyages, it was impossible to sleep. After a few days, Claus could not bear it anymore and asked me if he could go to a hotel to sleep. Of course, I accepted.

It was the traditional main bath of all the swamis and sadhus of all the Akhadas that made our trip so enjoyable and memorable. It completely wiped out all our discomfort. It was a magical moment, which I will never forget. Early in the morning, well before sunrise, all the naked sadhus assembled, arranged by the Akhada. We were told to stand in groups of four, hold hands and form a procession, headed by two or four richly adorned horses with a naked sadhu sitting on each, who were beating a huge drum, or blowing into a long circular trumpet. The horses preceded the Mahant (Head of the Akhada), who sat in a box on top of a heavily decorated elephant. We, the members of each Akhada, followed him. We were all covered with ash and were given a *mala* (garland) of marigolds.

There were so many of us and of so many types — chubby, very thin, massive, well-built bodies, tall, small, from young to very old. We all sported long hair, some people had very long hair indeed and others sported matted locks. Some walked with a cane and some with a *trishul* (trident) or a sword or spear, others with nothing in their hands.

The procession was very long and the Akhadas were placed according to their importance and seniority. I believe the order of placement had been a bone of contention and had led to heated arguments between senior Akhadas. The issue seemed to have been settled somehow.

Claus, Ani, and Sunny, were not swamis, and therefore were not allowed to participate in this procession (*pradakshina*). We walked — 1,00,000 men — hand in hand on the road, naked, barefoot, and covered with ash and marigold adorned necks. The huge multicoloured crowd around us sang, prayed, and tried to break the police cordon to touch us, surrounded by a huge golden cloud of dust. They threw marigold flowers or coins on us, while the trumpets blared and the drums beat into my ears... it was an incredible experience. I felt as though I had gone back to the days of antiquity, somewhere many millennia ago, yet we were on the threshold of the 21st century. At last, we reached the main bathing spot, Har Ki Pauri, the holiest spot on the Ganga in Haridwar.

We all quickly dipped into the water as soon as the head priest announced the auspicious moment for us to do so. As soon as the bath was over, we covered ourselves with ash again and rejoined our procession to take us back to the point of departure. As we were leaving, the next Akhada entered the holy waters. As we were proceeding towards our final destination I noticed Claus, Ani, and Sunny making desperate gestures to attract my attention.

Finally, understanding that something was wrong, I went towards the barricade along the road where they told me that trouble was brewing. As the people at the tail-end of my akhada were stepping out of the holy waters, the people standing at the forefront of the next akhada, waiting for their turn, had started a fight. They were using their swords, spears, and whatever they could lay their hands on. They resented having been told to take their bath *after* our Akhada... how unholy! We ran away and tried to find our Akhada's headquarters. We were not the only ones running away as we saw horse-mounted policemen charging towards us and hitting sadhus with their *lathis* (canes).

We were desperately looking for a place to hide. Imagine me, a white naked Western swami, covered in ash, running in the streets of a city, trying to save his skin along with that of his friends. We were frantic and panicking. All doors and shops were closed save for that of a milk vendor who was hurriedly closing his shutters. Despite his refusal to help us, we forced ourselves into his shop and then let him close it. We could see through narrow gaps, naked swamis running as fast as they could with the police pursuing them and hitting them.

Surprisingly, calm was restored in no time and the town looked as though nothing had happened. No bus or tyres were set ablaze and no shops looted, as is usually done elsewhere on such occasions. All the shops re-opened. It was business as usual and we went looking for our Akhada's headquarters where we were given some sweets.

We returned to our camping site, exhausted, and dazed by such an awesome and later scary experience. Reporters were happily interviewing celebrities from far away lands, who had come to the Mela for the event of the century. Of course, the international press covering the event gobbled this fight up, clicking away, and filming the incident. It certainly makes for an interesting subject, showing the modern world those hordes of mad naked men charging towards another group of mad naked men, the blood flowing from their bodies.

Once all our emotions were spent, we decided to go the next day to the Himalayas to calm our minds.

30

AUM SHANTI SHANTI SHANTI

My brother Gerard had always helped me a lot during all the years I spent in India. He really loved me as he felt that I had dared to achieve things he could have only dreamt about. He had chosen stability and the safety of a Government job even though he was extremely good in English and many other subjects. He was very affectionate towards our mother, who during the years I was in India, worried about me and frequently urged me to return, especially after my divorce and when I lost my job.

My brother's health deteriorated fast and the metastasis spread throughout his body, reaching the vertebrae and the central nervous system. He was in such horrible pain that not even morphine could alleviate his pain. I was at the Allahabad Kumbh Mela in January 2001. Something told me that I should carry my cellular phone with me.

After four days at the Kumbh Mela, I got a call from my sister. She said that Gerard had passed away. I was speechless. I became like a zombie and let my people take me away. Jayapalan, my friend and associate since my struggling days, joined me in Delhi and we both caught a plane the same evening. I boarded the plane still dressed in my *dhoti*, my *malas* (Indian rosary) of Rudrakshas (the seed from the Rudraksha tree), and my body covered with ash.

I arrived just in time to be present for the funeral in the Church of Serignan, Gerard's village. My sister-in-law asked me to say something in the church and in this 1500-year-old church, I sang one of the most beautiful Hindu prayers —

Aum, asatoma Satgamaya tamosoma Jyothir gamaya.
Mrityor ma amritam gamaye.
Aum Shanti, Shanti, Shanti

This roughly means —

Aum, lead us from untruth to truth,
From darkness to light,
From Death to Life.
Aum, Peace, Peace, Peace

The church was full. I translated the song into French for my family and everybody there, all his friends, all the civil servants who had worked with him for nearly 30 years, and his friends from the Police Department who had enjoyed his warmth, his affection, and his unfailing willingness to help anyone who would ask him. Then the priest pronounced his homily, an admirable and simple one, where he talked about death bringing everyone together regardless of religion... When I think about it now, tears come to my eyes.

After the ceremony, I brought our mother back home and she kept saying, 'Why him, why are my sons going away so soon and why must I stay here?'

She was 88 years old then and I could not answer her question, as there was no answer… we have no hold over our death, or birth.

Spiritually, she would not have understood anything regarding this. I had no answer but to hug her tight and make her feel that we, my loving younger sister and I, were still with her, even if I was so far away.

My brother's death shattered my mother. She lost her wits and became forgetful. She kept hearing sounds and complained that our neighbours were too noisy during the night and played loud music, when there was no one staying in the house near ours. She would also sometimes forget to switch off the gas stove. She frequently fell on the floor like a wooden log. Thankfully, she didn't have osteoporosis, and never broke a bone.

We had to do something, as she could no longer stay alone in her home. She did not want to leave the house, which they had struggled so much to buy on my father's meagre salary. My sister-in-law who had promised her husband, my brother Gerard, that she would look after her after his death, proposed to take her to her own home. She was a nurse who had specialised in geriatrics and was the ideal person to take care of her.

Month after month, my mother's Alzheimer's progressed to a point where she was not able to recognise me when I came back from India. She would look at me blankly, not responding to my questions. Arlette, my sister-in-law, would say to her, 'Mamy Fabre, *c'est* Christian.'

Silence... not a word from her... no more hugs from my mother, who now did not know who I was and could hardly talk... for me she was already dead! However, from time to time her memory would come back and she would dress up in the middle of the night and attempt to go out. She said it was time for her to go to school and that her mother was going to take her there. The last time I saw her alive, a sudden burst of memory came back to her and she asked me, 'Where are you going Christian?'

'I am going back to Chennai, Maman.'

'Be very careful and look after yourself.'

'Yes, Maman, I will...'

She had just turned 90 years old.

It is true that I am a Hindu monk, who according to some canons is supposed to have renounced the world. However, family is sacred for me as much as it is for most Indian families.

The *Vedas* (ancient Hindu scriptures) say —

Pitri Devo Bhava, Matri Devo Bhava, Guru Devo Bhava, Athithi Devo Bhava. (Your father is God, your mother is God, your guru is God, your guest is God).

I am also proud of my son, even though he left with his mother when he was just 8 years old. Life separated us and my poverty did not allow me to see him while he grew up, because she took him to Japan. Despite this distance and the rare meetings we have had during the past 35 years, I have always loved him and feel a deep attachment towards him. According to one of the correspondents for a foreign magazine in Singapore who had come to interview me, my son is now a renowned journalist.

Like everyone, even I have had my share of hard moments, but I found peace and acceptance in myself, loving myself for what I am and accepting everyone for what they are — human beings. I learnt this in India, without which I would not have been able to continue my life. I owe my knowledge to India and its remarkable people.

31

THE STORY OF DUDE

I came up with the idea of proposing our own exclusive collections to our foreign clients. They were out-sourcing the manufacturing of their products, but we thought they could pick up designs from us as well. For me it was a way of developing our business in addition to offering a better service to the client. I interviewed, hired, and put into place a new design department. Interestingly for us, it worked well and we are still offering our collections to our customers. It came to my mind that if our customers liked our collections, surely it would be well received in India also.

Since 1977, life had changed a lot in Indian cities. Thanks to television and other media, the boom of Information Technology and call centres, both employing millions of young, freshly educated, men and women, thirsty for new designs in western wear, and with lots of disposable income, we were assured that if our collections were well targeted, there would be success. Hence, we embarked on another project — creating our own brand.

Firstly, I had no idea what to call it, and secondly I did not know how I would finance it. Concerning the name of the brand, I decided to do it democratically.

I asked every one to come up with five names, write each one on a piece of paper and give it to Pinky, my personal secretary. We mixed them all up, and chose one. 'Dude' it said. We went for it as it certainly fit the attitude of our targeted customers who were between 18-30 years old. We registered it and as with all government processes in India, it took a very long time to find out that there was no objection to it. However, we were told it would take another year at least for the name to be exclusively acquired by us for the whole of India. As Fashions International was doing well, I could use part of its income to create another division, which I named StudioFI (FI for Fashions International).

We looked for a store and found one bang in the middle of an area where our target age group congregated in large numbers in Chennai — Besant Nagar, Elliot Beach. In the evenings, the whole area is crowded with youngsters and soon our Dude store became a landmark where they would meet. Thanks to an aggressive and expensive advertising campaign, our brand name was strategically located all over Chennai on huge billboards.

The store was doing well, our brand was well received all over India and was being sold through multi-brand outlets, when a Delhi court ordered us to stop selling our products (a stay order).

Another brand based in north India, objected to our using the word 'Dude' as they estimated this was phonetically too close to theirs. I have been assured that in any court of law in Europe such a judgment would immediately have been quashed and the case dismissed.

However, since copyright was new to India, there was no precedent for such cases. Though assured by the Judge that we would eventually be given a favourable judgment, he advised us to solve this issue amicably. We did not want to waste funds in such a matter, as it would have dragged on endlessly in court. Therefore, we had to stop marketing Dude. I was feeling totally at a loss about what to do, this setback was like an added weight on my back, along with other important issues, that called for my attention.

32

GURU-DISCIPLE RELATIONSHIP

In the olden days, one had to earn a Guru. Remember Swami Swayamprakash who had to wait nearly a week for his Guru to accept him as his disciple? My own Guru had his temperamental moments. Sometimes he taught me very nice things such as the Narayana Stotram, a beautiful *bhajan* which I sing every morning before my meditation and contemplation. It stays long in my heart and makes my day easier. On other days he did not even bother to smile at me and would send me back to Madras without a single word, just a wave of his hidden-in-ochre-coloured-cloth hand. Sometimes, my poor knowledge of the Tamil language, spoken by nearly 100 million people in the world, was a hindrance. Often, just sitting near him was enough to recharge my 'batteries' and I would return to Madras happy and fresh. Sometimes, I feel that I have learned much more from his silence than his words. Today, many think that a CD, a book on meditation or a self-styled guru is sufficient for them to reach the Ultimate.

I know of a so-called swami, a Westerner, who makes people pay him in dollars to have his *darshan*, what a shame.

Here in India, the Guru is considered a kind of doctor, who knows better than you what you are suffering from, who knows better than you do what the appropriate medicines are that you have to take.

Orders and advice given to one's disciples are meant to help, and not to fulfil the aspirations of a domineering person who wants to brainwash people. Even his apparent toughness is a form of Love.

The first thing I do when someone asks me if they can become my *shishya* is to find out if he has in him the determination to be a *sannyasin*, because it is a long, hard, and constraining path. I observe if this person is capable of humility and compassion, because as soon as he goes out of my sight he could behave in an arrogant manner or even be a very bad person. This has happened many times with some would-be disciples.

I remember a man from Denmark who, once I had left the hermitage, treated Sunny and Ruby as though they were his servants. I immediately showed him the way out of our ashram.

Then I watch carefully how the person meditates. If one cannot stay put and quiet for 20 minutes then how will he be able to live a life of non-attachment and contemplation? I look at his eyes after meditation and see lots of things in them. The eyes are the windows to the self.

If that person has passed the first test of meditation, then I give him elementary instructions —

- While in the ashram you will wear only those two white *dhoties* I am giving you now. White symbolises purity and the renouncing of the ego.
- You will walk barefoot while in our ashram so that you will have direct contact with Nature of which you are part and parcel.
- You will rise at daybreak and after your morning ablutions, you will clean the temple and decorate it with flowers especially grown for this purpose.
- You will always have a humble attitude and will take care of your Guru in the true sense of Indian traditions.
- During the day in the ashram, you will perform *seva.* That is physical work, which is an important part of your spiritual life. Peel vegetables, clean up the dining hall, work in the vegetable garden, or wash the dishes in the kitchen, etc. Not only will these activities teach you humility and patience, but also it will stabilise your ever-active mind and contribute to your spiritual progress.
- The disciple never fears his Guru and will have affection and respect for him.

He also has his *sadhana* to perform with me twice in a day.

He has to be on time, clean, and dressed in a fresh *dhoti*.

Physical cleanliness is very important in Hinduism because it reflects internal clarity. After having properly chanted 'Aum' thrice together, I review my *shishya's* progress and discuss with him whatever difficulties he may have encountered in his spiritual development, such as an overactive mental landscape, physical impatience, etc. I ask him to chant *japas* that he has to repeat many times during the day. Even though it may appear mechanical to recite *japas*, they have a particular mantric power. This means that the sounds that the *japas* consist of contribute to different states of consciousness in each disciple. Then, according to each disciple's progress, I give him a special mantra that will be specifically for him. For this occasion, a Brahmin priest will perform a special *puja*. Beforehand I explain to my would-be *shishyas* what it is all about so he understands the importance of such rituals, which have been performed for many millennia.

It is important for the would-be *shishyas* to understand that 'humans are not the centre of the world, but rather Nature is the centre of the world and humans are only part of the very same Nature. Hence, offerings to the sun, fire etc, are only ways of making an offering to Nature, which is nothing else but the Self, which we are.

Therefore, a Brahmin priest offering flowers, incense, and prayers, honours the five elements that constitute everything — fire, air, water, ether, and earth. I then ask him to read the sacred scriptures like the *Thirumantiram* by Tirumular, one of the most ancient sacred texts of Tamil Nadu (3rd century AD). This text says —

Heart and tongue in Unison met, The Lord cognise,
Though in diverse shapes He be, Him in unity find;
then, e'en though shaken in life like axle from pin,
Seek the Primal Lord in love and Him to yourself bind.

Or the *Avadhuta Gita*, the foundation of my Spirituality, my 'Bible' that I read regularly, has one of my favourite *shlokas* (stanzas) —

As the self is filled by the Self,
so all is filled continuously by you.
There is no meditator or meditation.
Why does your mind meditate shamelessly?

(Chapter I, Shloka 26. Translation by Swami Ashokananda of the Ramakrishna Mission, Madras, India)

How long does the initiation period, or preparation, last? It all depends on the will and the inner qualities of the aspiring *shishya.* One month? Three months? One year? Several years?

When I am satisfied with the progress of the student, his determination, his resolve, his faith, then I will tell him he is ready. We perform the Brahmachari Diksha in our temple while *pujaris* chant appropriate ancient Sanskrit texts, and perform the relevant puja.

The disciple will offer his Guru a copper plate filled with various seasonal fruits, a coconut that has been broken open, bananas, oranges, and at least a one-rupee coin. In ancient days, *shishyas* used to also offer cows, fortunately for the would-be *shishyas* those days are over. I then give him his name by tracing the name with my middle finger on a plate full of rice.

His name generally comes to me by observing the would-be *shishya* during the time he spends with me. It is the first step towards full *sannyas*. His new name will help him to associate himself not only with me, but also, and more importantly, with our core spirituality. In fact, to be a Brahmachari means that he is devoting himself completely to Brahman (the Primal Consciousness), the Supreme, the All, the Ultimate. Shiva, being one Aspect of Brahman, the Aspect of Auspiciousness. He undertakes to serve Brahman in the person of his Guru, to learn humility from his Guru, submission, compassion, patience, determination, and the abandonment of his ego.

In the old days, to emphasise his submission he had to wash his Guru's feet and cover them with sandal paste. I do not encourage such a practice. Finally, from now on, the *shishya* will not cut either his hair or his beard or moustache unless for a special condition, like my death, or for health reasons.

From this moment onwards, I teach him practices that we never reveal to non-initiated and unworthy persons. *Tapas*, austerity exercises, are not meant to expiate sins, but rather to control one's jealousy, anger, greed, etc. which multiplies the energy in one's body as well as frees and calms the mind. Tapas is performed while chanting *japas* with special mantras.

The *shishya's* Brahmachari period entirely depends on him. If he has a very strong ego, I wait for circumstances to erode it. It usually does not take very long because as soon as one treads on the spiritual path, lots of obstacles present themselves and make our progress difficult.

The obstacles however, help one learn more and help in finding ways to fight and reduce the importance of one's ego, and to move forward until this ego disappears. I will not say it is an easy thing to do. No. It is very difficult but it is an absolute must for a spiritual life and I am very strict about that. How do I evaluate the progress of the aspiring *sannyasin*?

Following a long stay at our ashram, I can judge him. Can he maintain the course of faith, and does he have determination during his *sadhana*, without which one cannot move forward on this path. If I notice that several doubts are overtaking his mind, if he cheats on the rigour and the regularity of his practice, I wait a little longer. I also ask Sunny to observe him when I am not in the ashram. Does he behave in the same manner as when I am there? I had an Indian disciple from Delhi, who once I was back to Madras, was relaxing and behaving as though he was on holiday there. When I returned I asked him to pack up and go back to where he came from.

Lastly, the most important condition for me to accept someone as my *shishya* and to get Sannyas Diksha from me is, that he should be at least 20 years old and both his parents must agree to it. If he is married, the case is more difficult and delicate and I should have his wife's agreement to it.

Then comes the time for the Sannyas Diksha (ceremony) which I too had to go through many years ago. First, a barber comes to the ashram to shave off the hair of the aspiring *sannyasin.* We perform this ceremony on the banks of a lake within our ashram's premises, often during Mahashivaratri, which takes place in January or February, the coldest time in our Hills.

He undresses fully and throws away all his clothes. Naked, he dips himself thrice in the lake. He walks naked to our temple and sits in front of me.

The *pujaris* perform his death ceremony and then his birth ceremony, at which point in time, his old self has been dissolved and a new self has come to life, then I give him his new name. If his Brahmachari name was for example Shankar, it will be removed and from then on, he will be known as Swami Shankarananada Brahmendra Avadhuta. Brahmendra is to indicate our lineage from Sadashiva Brahmendra and Avadhuta as his integration to the Avadhuta Sect, which means 'liberated soul', someone who has removed all obstacles and attachments to this world and moves on the path of a spiritual life. After this, I will whisper his personal definitive mantra into his ear, the one he will recite every day, the one he will use to give him strength when facing hardships. This mantra will be part of his life, will never leave him and could be easily recalled at any moment. At last, I give him two new ochre *dhoties* to wear when he is outside this ashram.

He will be allowed to live without clothes only in this ashram or the one he might create, or in places such as the Samadhi of his Gurus or temples dedicated to Dattatreya. Roaming naked everywhere is not recommended, as people may not understand the reason behind this.

Our last Guru before my own, Swayamprakash Brahmendra Avadhuta, used to roam naked everywhere and had stones thrown at him while he was walking through villages. The police arrested him often.

There comes a moment when there is nothing else to say to the new monk, but for him to continue his practice assiduously. I then give him the choice to stay with me, or to leave and found his own ashram, or to become a roaming monk on the roads of India, or anywhere in the world.

He will have to be careful to keep the purity of his non-attachment because it is easy to lose it. Without noticing, one's own resolve diminishes in strength.

In the very beginning the *shishyas* are full of enthusiasm, they meditate, they are full of devotion for their Guru and work hard, but with time and advancing age, they lose a lot of their ardour and relax their practices, or fall into a kind of spiritual routine without joy and full of ego.

The simplest of qualities such as feeling the joy of life disappear. There is a story of a swami, who after a long, hot, difficult journey on foot and wearing only a *langot* (a narrow piece of cloth that covers the private parts), reached a pond, such as is found in almost every village in India. It was near the end of the day and the water looked cool and appealing.

He decided to have a bath in this pond. He went into the water with delight and started to scrub his body with the leaves of a nearby Neem tree (a very common tree in India known for its antiseptic properties). In the pond, he removed his *langot* and decided to clean it. He did so and spread it on a hot stone to dry. He swam around enjoying this relaxing time.

Meanwhile a rat took the *langot* away. The swami was unhappy with the state of affairs. He decided to stay in the village for some time (only three days are allowed by his Order) and with the alms he got he bought another *langot*, and for guarding it, he got a cat. He thought about the fact that he had to feed the cat and for this purpose, he begged a bit more and with the proceeds bought himself a cow for milk. Days passed by and he realised he could not look after this cow himself. He then decided to hire a woman to look after it, take it to graze, milk it, etc. The woman was very pretty and attractive... he married her... end of the *sannyasin*. He had lots of children... bye-bye to the *langot* and his non-attachment and the Ultimate. He had forgotten everything.

It is therefore important that the disciple abandons his ego and follows his Guru's instructions. Otherwise, he could find himself in difficult situations. I have seen many *sannyasins* blinded by their own ignorance, who believe they have reached the 'realisation'.

An ashram cannot exist unless there is an enlightened Guru

at its helm. Unfortunately, once the Guru attains *samadhi*, a follower is designated as the new head. Soon, the new head Guru will set up new rules and create regulations, and establish 'sins' where none were, and creates Paradises and Hells. This is how religions are built.

Disciples always ask me, 'How long will it take me to reach the Awareness of who I really am?'

I answer them, 'It can take a few minutes, few months, few years... or never. It can take a fraction of a tenth of a second. You will work hard on that. You will ask questions to your Guru. You will doubt. Then, suddenly, without warning, the dark cloud will tear away and everything will be clear. You will be aware that every atom and the space between the atoms of your body, and outside your body, is Consciousness. *You will know who you are.* Nothing will look the same after this. A difficult moment will look different. Problems will simply become situations. It does not mean you will never have challenging moments. After all, you have your Karma to go through, but solutions to your situations will come to you more easily. One thing is sure, once you have cognised this Awareness, your recognition will never leave you. A Guru's duties are to take you step by step towards your goal, but the last steps have to be taken by the *shishya*. The Guru can only point you towards the right direction and cannot be held responsible if you go in the opposite direction.'

My Guru's direct answers to my questions helped me a lot. His aura, his way of answering my questions, without any hesitation, was the key to my being strong enough to go through so many hardships to walk on my chosen path. This didn't mean that I didn't have doubts in my mind. I wondered, could my Guru make mistakes? The important thing is not only the teaching itself, but rather how the *shishya* will put it into practice. The Guru shows you the way.

If you make a mistake, the Guru cannot be held responsible. Do not judge your Guru. The Guru can have apparent defects; maybe he does not look like a Guru. He could be a man eaten up by leprosy, like my own Guruji. The *Avadhuta Gita* says —

Of the teacher — even if he be young, illiterate,
or addicted to the enjoyment of sense objects,
even if he be a servant or a householder —
none of these should be considered.
Does anyone shun a gem fallen in an impure place?'
'In such case one should not consider even the quality of scholarship.
A worthy person should recognise only the essence.
Does not a boat, though devoid of beauty and vermillion paint,
nevertheless ferry passengers?

(Chapter II, Shlokas I and II, *Avadhuta Gita*)

(Translated by Swami Ashokananda and published by the Ramakrishna Mission Madras, India)

I was shocked when I met Swami Sarveswara, my Guruji, for the first time, and I thought, how could this man be my Guru? He is physically handicapped. He cannot move freely and lives in such a sordid environment, how can he have so much beauty, such an aura around himself?

In the West, we are often weary of Gurus, as we are always afraid to lose our own free will. With my Guruji, it was never like that. I always questioned him and he was very patient with me and gave me answers I did not expect, so simple and yet so self-evident. I always remained the master of my own mind and I was never influenced to do things against my will.

Later on, if you become a Guru, you should also give your *shishya* the freedom to choose his path.

By the way, the best Gurus are those who teach in silence. Lord Shiva is also represented as the Ultimate Guru, sitting silent, facing south (Dakshinamurthy — *dakshina* - south, *murthy* - god) and teaching his disciples in silence (the four Rishis).

Your faith is also your free will. Real faith is never blind because it is based on an intuition that is worthy knowledge. Later on, time and happenings will strengthen your intuitions.

The Avadhuta, alone, pure in evenness of feelings,
abides happy in an empty dwelling place,
Having renounced all, he moves about naked.
He perceives the absolute, the All within himself.

(Chapter I, Shloka 73, Dattatreya's *Avadhuta Gita*)

I had the following questions in my mind while my Guruji taught me and I am sure that my present *shishyas* must have similar ones.

Can a Guru be wrong?

Can a religion be true? Here again, one has to use reason and one's own judgement.

If you have learnt enough from your Guru, if you have read enough about his teachings, if your reasoning tells you only one answer, which has to be a frank and definite '*Yes*', then go for him, adopt him, or rather let him adopt you. If after serious thinking, and reasoning, you are firmly of the conviction that this is the religion you want to follow, then go ahead, regardless of the religion — Hinduism, Christianity, Islam, or anything else. Be careful though of intolerance in all its forms, as it is the seed of discord, war, and all death. A real Guru never hits a table with his fist to prove a spiritual point. He never threatens you. He never forces you to do something you do not want to do, or to believe in something that goes against your inner feelings. A true Guru uses his and your common sense, as the Ultimate is and has always been simple and within you.

Nisargadatta Maharaj, a revered 20th century Hindu Saint from Mumbai used to say, 'Religions are a heap of words and are man-made. Spirituality, however, is God made.'

To become a spiritual person is not an opportunity that is given to everyone and requires the aptitude for self-inquiry. For others, religions are here to help them walk on to the spiritual path, as it is more within the common man's intellectual reach.

Today, everyone puts the name of God everywhere except in the right place where It should be. Unfortunately, swamis, sadhus, or mystics of various denominations are power hungry and have built empires with money taken from their devotees and disciples who are desperately seeking Knowledge. This Knowledge however, is very simple and yet so powerful, so close to you.

Nisargadatta Maharaj said, '*You Are That*.'

I shall always cherish the following *shlokas* from the *Avadhuta Gita* —

In my mind there is neither the meditator,
meditation, nor the object of meditation.
Thou hast no samadhi.
There is no region outside thee,
nor is there any substance or time.
I am the nectar of Knowledge, homogeneous existence, like the sky.

Chapter III, Shloka 41, *Avadhuta Gita*

During the last 15 years, I have had many visitors and would-be *shishyas*, yet I cannot say that I have found the one who will take over once I am gone. My Guruji used to say, 'You will have to go through 1,00,000 would-be *shishyas* to find the one who will be the best.'

They all want to get instant Knowledge, instant consciousness, like instant coffee powder on which we pour some hot water, stir it well, and you got it! They want to have a quick answer to all their problems.

When I tell them that they have their answers in themselves, they are puzzled and cannot understand what I am talking about. Some come here as if to a holiday resort and soon I have to tell them to leave. Some come out of curiosity and soon go. What they find difficult is that when they are in the middle of nature, contemplating, they come face to face with themselves. They do not like this because they cannot cope with it and therefore, they run away. Some people are seeking a place where they will find free lodging and food, and are upset when we ask them to contribute toward the expenses as it is expressly mentioned in our website *www.aumnamahshivaya.org.in.* Some get married and others have mental disorders. Some cannot understand that no ritual is necessary to reach the Ultimate, because they expect to perform pujas, sing endlessly, burn oil lamps, mumble mantras, etc. Since they do not find that here, they run away. Some do what I call spiritual window shopping, going from one ashram to another until they are thrown out, or leave when they don't like it.

Therefore, I have decided not to look actively for *shishyas* anymore. I have also decided to call our ashram a 'hermitage' and accept only those in whom I sense some similar feelings — the search for the knowledge of the Ultimate.

33

A BUCKET FULL OF HOLES

September 11, 2001 was a blow to our company. All our foreign customers assured us that nothing would affect our business, but when they did place their orders, the quantity was slashed considerably and our company was endangered. We suddenly had to squeeze finances everywhere and ensure that there was no waste at all. It was difficult, but the situation soon got better and we saw a big increase in our turnover.

But, something continued to trouble me, I realised that I was the only motor running this company. It meant that I always had to see ahead and have ideas that would propel us forward, or find solutions in difficult situations. I was yearning to increase the number of days spent in our hermitage and wanted to distance myself from the business. The question that would always arise in my mind was who will lead next? Of course, Jayapalan was very much with me and I would ensure that he carry more responsibilities on his shoulders, but with our company's growth, it needed a more structured set-up.

I had to find someone to take over my responsibilities. I started to look for that person. A few years passed by and though our business grew considerably, our net profit was not matching it. I knew that I had to bring about changes, but how should I do that?

People hate change and as Mahatma Gandhi said, 'If you need changes, you must first change.'

I called in a financial advisor to go through our books and after two months of work, he said, 'Your company is like a bucket full of holes and one is the biggest of them all. Plug that big hole first and your company will be back on its feet and later on you will be able to plug the smaller holes.' The big hole he referred to was one of my employees who got the biggest percentage of our revenues.

Anita got the biggest percentage of commission on our revenues, because she was one of the first people to join us. Years passed us by and from the 20,000 pieces of our first season's orders, we were now dealing with about 4 million pieces. Of course, her income followed the same upward curve.

Unbeknownst to me, Anita was telling people that she was the CEO of the company. She neglected the department I had entrusted her with. Whatever work took place, was without her involvement. Our executives were doing the job without her. Although she was aware of and understood the financial difficulties we were facing at that time, she did not make any move to help us by coming forward to reduce the huge package she was taking home (without even deserving it).

As she was also taking credit for the performance of our executives, resentment grew amongst all the employees and they ostracised her.

She finally understood that she was not wanted anymore within our company and was despised by everyone, so she asked me to relieve her of her post, which I happily did. Thanks to that, today, two years after her resignation we are still alive, functioning, and growing despite the 2008-09 world financial turmoil we are facing.

Unfortunately, this means that I cannot spend as much time as I used to in our hermitage, as I had to take all the duties into my own hands once again.

Economically things are very difficult at present, but we feel the team spirit of our company's staff behind us, supporting us even during this terribly difficult time and I am sure we shall prevail. It is a comfort to feel everyone's concern.

I feel vulnerable with my lack of formal knowledge in terms of management, specifically in terms of personnel management, and financial management. Nevertheless, I let myself be guided by my understanding of human nature, which is no different from my own. I go by the understanding that humans are capable of the most beautiful actions and even the most horrible ones. In between those extremes, there are billions of variations. In fact, each individual is a variation of those extremes. Therefore, whatever happens either in my personal, spiritual or professional life, I take it as it comes. I would forgive anyone's actions immediately. This does not mean that I forget. If we know that a dog is dangerous and can bite you any time, we do not go near it.

The same goes for humans. After all, they are nothing more than an integral part of Nature.

How could I go through this turmoil, looking after the entire company's needs and yet not forgetting my Awareness? How could I keep my calm and balance when everything seemed to converge to make my life more difficult?

I have a habit of leaving the door to my office open to make it easy for anyone to come and talk to me. I have to listen, understand, comfort and help all those who come to me as they know that whatever they say will be in confidence and that I will try everything possible to help them, whether the problem is professional or personal. Like a loan without interest required for building a home, or funds for school admission, lending a patient ear to someone who has had a fight with a wife, or helping one look for a child that has run away. Sometimes, I feel this is too heavy on me and I must admit I wish I could just drop everything and run away, but I know that I must keep my commitment towards them and I go on.

My Guruji told me, 'You should now spend one week in

Madras and three weeks in your hermitage.' I wonder if my associate, Jayapalan, and everyone in our company and the customers will accept this way of running our company.

I know they are all attached to me, but I have now been living and working in India for the past 30 years and for the last 30 years, I have been selling India to the world. Surely, it should give me some peace and rest now?

34

LIFE IN OUR HERMITAGE

My Guruji had asked me to build our ashram temple and gave me all the dimensions that the Shiva Lingam should have, as well as the many rules under which I should have it made and what I should name it.

'You will call it Jyothirlingeshwar (the Lord Shiva Lingam of Light) and it must be 12 fingers long. You will place under it nine precious stones, and you will ensure it faces the East.'

I followed my Guruji's wishes and the Lingam is now in an exquisite, spotlessly clean white temple, like a jewel case. On the left of the Shiva Lingam, I have installed a 3 ft statue of Bikshudhanar (Lord Shiva shown as a naked beggar), a replica of a 12th century Kumbakonam statue that is now in the Madras Museum. On the right side, is a 5 ft statue of Dattatreya, the semi-mythical Sage who is often represented as a naked mendicant, with three heads and six arms. The heads represent Brahma (God of Creation), Vishnu (God of Preservation), and Shiva (God of Destruction).

This in fact is an allegorical representation of the Ultimate. On the wall behind the Shiva Lingam, there is a painted representation of my vision at Vridhuchalam.

Behind our hermitage there is a little hill overlooking the whole valley. I had a *mandapan* built on top and installed a superb Shiva carved from a two-and-a-half ton single piece of marble. It was a tremendous job to have it installed there. First, I had it made in Jaipur (Rajasthan) and transported to our hermitage, which stands at an altitude of 1300 metres. We had to use a huge wench to manoeuvre it into position, but once there, it is simply splendid and going up there, spending hours contemplating the sunset is a wonderful experience that many of my visitors like to enjoy. Sitting up there and looking at our hermitage I enjoy looking at the 10,000 silver oak tress we have planted there, with pepper creepers all over them and our coffee, which has received awards and brings in an income for Sunny.

I can see many flowers around our buildings and the dark grass grown in the shape of the holy word 'Aum' that Sunny and his nephew had created on the front lawn. We have planted many species of trees and I can see the vegetable garden where we cultivate most of our needs — lettuce, big fleshy tomatoes, spinach, leeks, cabbages, thyme, and rosemary. We also have olive trees and cypresses like those in the south of France.

A company that manufactures aeroplanes, rockets, and tanks had invited me to give a lecture to CEOs during a seminar in a Renaissance-era castle outside Bordeaux in France. My secretary, Pinky, negotiated that in return they donate a complete solar power panel system to the hermitage.

I am very interested in and amazed by Internet Technology. Our Fashions International customers use it extensively. At our hermitage, we have no telephone line and there is no signal tower for cellular phones, we are completely isolated from the external world.

But, because I need to keep track of business, I have a satellite dish antenna that allows me to connect to the World Wide Web. It allows me to chat with my staff in Chennai and my would-be disciples all over the world. In a room next to our temple, I have installed a desk where I can answer my chats and e-mails, and re-read my many spiritual books. On the other side of the courtyard of our temple is my room. A thin mattress on a grass mat and walls painted ochre.

Spiritual visitors also flock to our hermitage. Sometimes, no one would come for a week and then the next week we would get busloads of people. I dread the visitors who come in large groups, as they do not all come for a spiritual purpose. Often they are just curious and want to see the *Vellakaran Swami* (white-skinned Swami).

Families drop by to take their *aashirwad* (blessing) from the swami. Some do visit me to quench their genuine spiritual thirst. I always wish to receive those people, but they are so few. I prefer to be left alone to contemplate nature around me, but my Guruji once told me, 'You must allow anyone to come and visit you. Rich or poor, highly placed, or simple folks, nice people, or ruffians, they are all the Ultimate. And who knows, maybe you will find the one person who will be the real seeker."

My life at our hermitage is simple. I wake up early morning and after my ablutions, I proceed to apply three lines of ash on several parts of my body and my *bindu* (red dot) on my forehead — all the signs of a follower of Lord Shiva. Why ash? Ash is a symbol of life and death and a reminder of the ephemeral side of our existence. The three lines remind us of the three *gunas*, the three principles that govern our life – desire (*rajas*), inertia (*tamas*) and spirituality (*satva*). Doraiswami would already have cleaned the temple, washed it with clean water and applied the three horizontal lines of ash to the Shiva Lingam, applied the kumkum (red powder) *bindu* and decorated the Lingam with fresh flowers that we grow especially for this purpose.

Once the temple is ready, I start my *sadhana*, which I would end with a *japa* (chanting) of *Aum Namah Shivaya.* It takes me at least half an hour to do that, I then stand up and walk around the Shiva Lingam clock-wise. This action implies that the Shiva Lingam is the centre of the universe and we are small specks walking around it. One has to be humble. I end this by prostrating in front of the Shiva Lingam. Unfortunately, I cannot share the meaning of everything I practise, unless I am with my disciples, as this has to be transmitted to a 'worthy' person.

I then go to our dining room where Sara, our faithful cook is waiting for me to take my breakfast along with the residents. We have a vegetarian meal with Indian dishes and end with a cup of our own organic coffee outside, with everyone sitting around me. We talk about many subjects and our conversation invariably ends with some spiritual topic. If we have a visitor, he would ask a question that he would like answered.

If they are of a personal nature, he would wait till I am available to hear him or her out in private. I make sure that I am always available and reachable. Everyone likes this, but it is sometimes a heavy burden for me to carry. I find less and less time for myself, but nature is here all around me and this makes my life easier as I am Nature. I am part of it all... no, I *am* Nature, I *am that.*

After our little discussion over steaming cups of coffee, everyone is free to follow their own pursuits, reading, trekking, or simply going up to our *mandapan* for meditation or contemplation. The stunning view from up there makes it difficult to leave this place. As for me, I go to my study adjoining our temple and opposite the inner courtyard to my bedroom. There I open my laptop and my Firefox browser to see my online newspapers, the *Midi Libre* (a Southern French daily), *Le Monde*, *The New York Times*, *The Washington Times*, *The Guardian*, and of course, *The Indian Express.*

I feel it is important for me to know what is happening in this mad, mad, world economy, as politics really influences it a lot and can make it a terrible place to live in. I have to keep myself tuned in to what is happening so that I can manage our company properly. My Yahoo Messenger as well as Skype opens automatically as I start working, and I can see who is present in our office, 400 km away. Once I have read all the e-mails that have accumulated since the previous night, I do that 'diagonally' as there are too many of them — around 1900 per day. I answer all those I think deserve, or require to be answered. I read a few interesting articles on some websites, either with a spiritual or business subject, or I look around networking websites and meet new people from around the world.

35

CHRISTIAN FABRE

As we could not continue selling our own collection under the name 'Dude', since it would amount to contempt of court, which is a serious offence, and even more so if a foreigner is involved, we had to quickly find another name and build a whole new brand.

Once again, I decided to opt for a democratic process for finding a new brand name. Very soon my staff came back and told me, 'Swamiji, we have unanimously found a new name for our brand.'

'Which name have you chosen?'

They looked at me, smiled and said, 'Yours! Christian Fabre!'

I was taken aback at first. This was so unexpected, Christian Fabre is a name only used on official papers since my Guruji gave me the name Swami Prananvananda Brahmendra Avadhuta. But, I accepted their decision.

We changed a lot of things in the process. We created a private limited company along with Jayapal as it would facilitate getting bank finances more easily and would considerably reduce the weight of responsibilities on my head alone.

We also decided to change our commercial policy and stopped selling through multi-brand outlets or distributors who were eating up most, and sometimes all, of our profit margin. We started our own chain of exclusive Christian Fabre outlets.

The 2008-09 financial meltdown all over the world, made our international business more and more difficult as our customers faced the worst ever crisis they had to in more than 60 years. I knew that because India has a strong tradition of spending internally and does not entirely depend on exports, it would be able to face the situation much better than the West and USA. I knew that working with 400 million Indians who have the purchasing power, though somewhat eroded, would certainly be better than doing business with below zero GDP countries.

Having given most of our revenues to our staff for the past 21 years, our financial reserves are very thin. Banks are helping us now and we are on the track to recovery, since after five months of launching our first store we are now opening our seventh store in Chennai and the first one in Bengaluru. Our plan is a target of 50 stores by the end of 2010, and 150 by 2012.

When our Designs Department was created, I wondered

how to keep abreast with the latest fashion in order to give our customers ever-new products. I could of course, subscribe the department to the best fashion forecasting websites, but it would cost us a fortune. Therefore, I came up with the idea that I should bring the most important people in our Design Team to Europe and visit the important Fashion Fairs. Of course, when I voiced my idea they all jumped with joy. As Ani has had the experience of driving in Europe with me when he was my personal assistant, I decided to make him part of the travelling group, and he became the Graphic Designer. It was rewarding for them on two fronts — one, because they were able to see fashion in the streets of France, Spain, and Italy and see what the important European brands are up to in the fairs we attended. Secondly, it is the dream of all designers, or of anyone, to walk the streets of Paris, Rome, and Barcelona. Surely, not many young Indian men are fortunate enough to be able to do that twice a year. Staying in five-star hotels and driving rented cars, is certainly not what the average Indian man can afford to do. The designers are also entitled to pocket money to make some personal purchases they wish to bring back to their relatives back in India.

36

SKY-CLAD

As soon as I reach our hermitage, I promptly remove the two pieces of ochre cloth that cover my body. I fold them and put them aside. I shall wear them again only to go back to 'civilisation', to the plains, and up to Chennai. If a rare visitor is not warned before he comes to our hermitage, he is shocked on seeing me and does not know where to rest his eyes. But after a while, he is back to normal and leaves happy and contented, or puzzled if he has not understood the spirituality I follow. Although during the many years that I have been an Avadhuta Swami, I have never had a negative response. I feel that is due to the fact that I live my nakedness in a very natural way. After all, we are born without clothes and leave this life without them. When our last moment comes, we never take anything with us, even though the people left behind, always dress the departed before the cremation, or burial. Social laws do not govern a *sannyasin's* life, as he is outside the laws that govern society.

Naked swamis have always existed in India. Alexander the Great mentions that he encountered a swami, sitting still wearing not a stitch of clothing. He did not even bother to stand up for the Emperor of the Greeks.

Other invaders have come to Bharat and brought along several changes in society. Muslim invaders and Christian missionaries of so many denominations came along with the invaders and told Indian society how to behave with one another by imposing their laws. Even today, in the 21st century, the Indian Penal Code contains 350-year-old laws that have long ago been abolished in the countries they originated in.

For an Avadhuta Swami, being nude is a *tapas*. It cannot be taken with a Christian understanding of erasing sin, or seeking God's pardon. Hindus of our Spirituality do not accept the concept of sin, which is a rather Semitic idea. Hindus believe in Karma, for every action there is a re-action, there will be a punishment for a bad action, or a reward for a good one.

We are responsible for our lives, and the Ultimate has given each one of us everything we need to make our life good, even if we are born into it according to our past actions. At the beginning, I felt awkward and was worried about what people would think. I was able to get used to it soon and stopped worrying about it. I now live my nudity as an integral part of myself as I got rid of my inhibitions.

Understandably, the question that comes to mind for a Westerner is, 'But, why nudity?' So, let me explain it this way. Clothing is used for three purposes only —

- Since a *sannyasin* has vowed non-attachment to belongings, where is the need to show to which level of society one belongs?

  Your ego tells you to appear rich even when you cannot afford it. The *sannyasin's* life is geared towards annihilation of his ego, so why wear *dhoties* of silk or cotton decorated with intricate designs of gold or silver. A Dighambara is someone dressed with the four winds (four directions).

- To hide parts of your body that are important for the human species to reproduce. One is born naked and cannot take clothing along, after he dies. Since all men and all women are born with the same attributes, where is the need to hide what everyone knows? Semitic religions instil in human minds the concept of sin and that sexual relationships outside marriage is sin. Thanks to the zeal of Christian missionaries one believes that a Dark Age has befallen the Western world, in India and elsewhere, but before these ideas came to India, the existence of the *Kama Sutra* and the depiction of the statues in Kajuraho temples were there for all to see and admire.

- To protect you against cold, heat, or rain. An Avadhuta Swami is one with Nature and nothing separates him from Nature. It is only during inclement atmospheric elements that he should cover himself. He is not to succumb to the pride of owning this or that sexual attribute. Dattatreya, the first of our lineage Order, had 24 Gurus. They were all part of Nature.

He learned from a snake, from the sky, an ant, the stars, from the flowers, and the dogs that were always with him, he never found any of them covered! According to our Lineage Order, sexuality is something that one has to control and not necessarily destroy; trying to do so would be like imprisoning it in a house. When the doors are closed, Kama (God of Pleasures) would escape through the windows. If you closed the doors and windows, it would escape through the chimney. Closing the whole house would make it explode... instead, it is better to know Kama and control it and channel it and not be attached to it. Sexuality is energy. It is you, and should not be discarded, instead, it should be carefully managed and channelled for a positive purpose.

This body is only an illusion, why hide an illusion? Nothing is Real if it is destined to disappear once it reaches the end of its lifespan. Why hide what is not real? What is the body anyway? This envelope could appear handsome or pretty, but will it last?

As beautiful as it may look, this envelope is only a sack full of viscera and bones that one day will disintegrate into the basic elements to form another form or the same one...

I am often asked if the nudity of a *sannyasin* is not an anachronism in our 21st century. Why should I conform to the general way of dressing up? Or undressing? Why should I wear a tie? Why should I wear trousers and shoes?

Should I do it because everyone else does? Everybody wants to appear what he or she is not. Rare are those who do not. If I am to be called a non-conformist, let it be and if I am not, let that also be. When I reach our hermitage, I remove my *dhoti* and I put aside all 'appearances' — the useless and the superficial — and go back to Nature who I have never ceased to be. For me one thing is sure — in another 100 years, the naked sadhus of India, to whom I belong, will still exist and will continue to exist as they have been for nearly 5000 years now. Pharaohs have disappeared, Sumerians exist only in history books, but we will continue to exist.

I should be careful not to spread this naked sadhu culture too much, if everyone were to throw away their clothes, our clothing industry would go out of business! Here in India, being a naked *sannyasin* and being called the 'naked emperor of the ready-to-wear industry' does not shock anyone.

A French swami isn't surprising anymore. Even if I feel close to my country of birth, I do not feel it much. After all, my Sannyas Diksha ceremony has put an end to my first birth and given me a new birth into a new life. My white skin is visible to all, but this is the Maya (illusion) that makes them interpret their retina's perceptions as the truth. But in fact, they are seeing a white man whose body is actually an illusion created by Energy which is All, The Ultimate.

The Westerners see the Frenchman. The Indians see first the swami, the sage, the one who has The Awareness, and the Universal Guru in me. They naturally prostrate and touch my feet. A Westerner would think, look a white man who acts like a Guru...

If you perceive only this, please note that you cannot see any further than the tip of your nose. I see the human being, Shiva, the Ultimate in each one of us. I do not see the expensive and branded clothes he or she wears. I do not see an Indian, or an African, or a Frenchman; it is the consciousness of each one that counts. It is not important whether he or she is the Prime Minister of a country, or a *sadhu* covered in ash. The person in front of me could be a starving farmer whose harvest has been devastated by drought, or someone who is covered with Rudraksha *malas* (holy beads used by the Shivaites), linked with thick gold chains. What will anybody take away with them when they die? Nothing! They will not need them in their tomb. Their relatives will fight over its possession before the body grows cold.

Today, there are many men like me in India, despite the hard work put in by certain Christian Missionaries of a certain denomination. Let me tell you what happened to me. One day in December, during the monsoon, I was in the hermitage. It was cold and it was raining heavily.

Everyone had gone to a small town 20 km away and I was alone, reading peacefully, hearing only the raindrops falling heavily on the ground and then suddenly, I heard a strange sound from the road, far away from my room. I picked up an umbrella, and walked towards the road. I saw a jeep-like vehicle with a loudspeaker mounted on top. A man was screaming at the top of his voice on the microphone, exhorting me to go back to the folds of his Christian faith. I was the only human in a 10 km radius and to whom was he preaching? When I told him this, he increased the volume of his microphone. I turned around and left him to his schizophrenic ramblings. He went on and on, on his own, alone in the cold rain.

Whether you are a preacher or a mendicant, Bill Gates, or a call centre employee in India, a scientific researcher, or a housewife, a musician or a Bollywood actor, one is only Consciousness.

Consciousness of who he is, is what the true disciple has to develop in himself, the consciousness of Being and not 'appearing to be'. A popular wise saying tells us, 'Seeing is believing'. It is not however a question of seeing with the physical eyes, but rather with the eyes of the Ultimate in oneself. Some religions call it the Soul. In fact, it is very important to ask oneself questions. They will always lead you to the same answer — I am not. Am I this body? No, I am not. It is only an illusion as it is destined to disappear, etc. As you keep asking yourself questions, the answer will be the same — I am not.

– Who am I really? Why Life? Why Death? Why suffering?

These are the questions that everyone asks themselves at some point in their life. It is during a few short moments that one is given a glimpse of the answers, or rather The Answer — one is not the son of the Supreme, but one is part and parcel of the Supreme. This body and its surroundings is a reality that appears to be as it is, since it is not permanent.

These sparks of insight come to everyone and always leave a trace in one's heart. It can also be found by artists who are in essence very sensitive people and whose hearts vibrate more intensely than for the common person. Poets, painters, writers, musicians, and researchers have that 'divine' moment, that result in masterpieces or astounding discoveries.

We are living in an unreal world, but certain people create their own unreal worlds that exist only in their imagination. They create their own 'make believe' world. As long as they can live their dreams on the Internet, everything is great. Once they are face to face with the hard reality of things — *tapas*, *sadhana*, and solitude, they give up, as they find it too hard to go through. I tell my *shishyas*, 'You were born with the same opportunities as any other person on this planet. There are some who never notice them and die the same way they were born, wasting life as a human. Others see those opportunities, grab them, but let them go for many reasons, fear, mental weakness, etc. Some see those opportunities, grab them tightly and never drop one. The latter, are the ones who succeed. Which one do you want to be? It is a question of awareness and personal choice.

37

MY LIFE AND FRIENDS IN CHENNAI

In Chennai, the old Madras, the routine of my life changes completely. I am captured by the frenzy of the city, its noisy and polluted atmosphere and the burden of running a business. My home in Chennai is not mine, as I do not possess anything. It belongs to my associate, Jayapalan, who built it and offered me the use of the whole first floor. He lives on the ground floor, with his wife and children. The ambience is rather cosy, with the help of a few simple, inexpensive, but beautiful antique pieces of furniture we picked up from someone I know very well. Jayapalan offered me the first floor when he built the house, so we constructed it the way I wanted it. I had in mind the Roman Atrium and the Poddukottai (a city in south Tamil Nadu) architecture, where four wooden pillars would support a long tile-covered passage around a courtyard open to the sky. I filled it up with soil and planted a lovely garden. All the rooms open onto this inner garden, with large ceiling-to-floor glass doors.

It is especially pleasant during the monsoon where we can watch the rain falling on the small trees and plants in our courtyard. The spacious sitting room has very little furniture, but many cushions of several shades and hues from ochre to brown. A large flat screen TV is my luxury, which allows me to see what is happening in the world.

The satellite TV allows me to stay connected to France as I get TV5 Monde. On my old desk, in one corner of the room, my laptop is connected to the broadband Internet where I can chat and connect with my would-be or actual disciples from all over the world.

Rising at 6 a.m. in the morning, I sit in the veranda outside, surrounded by flowers, creepers, and tropical plants I have planted, a riot of colours shimmering in the morning sun. I have positioned them in such a way that nobody from the street or any of the neighbours can see me from their home. Though everyone knows I always live naked, I do not want to create any uneasiness. Anyway, the cook, Pongudi, takes care to inform everyone in the street of whatever is happening in my Chennai residence. I call her PBC — P for Pongudi, B for Broadcasting, C for Corporation.

I take my bath and apply my ash. In the meanwhile, a domestic help would have cleaned the room I use for my spiritual practices. He would have washed the Shiva Lingam and decorated it with flowers, lit the *deepam* (oil lamp), and planted the *agharbattis* (incense sticks). Once he has finished, I sit cross-legged in the Padmasana position on my *cusha* cross mat, spread on a low wooden *asana* (seat), facing the Shiva Lingam and perform my spiritual practices.

I then go back to my sitting room and read the newspapers, or read them online. Pongudi brings me a steaming cup of our prize winning ashram/hermitage plantation organic coffee. I enjoy these quiet moments, as they are so rare. In order to face the hard day ahead of us, a breakfast comprising typical South Indian dishes, shared with John, my personal assistant, follows.

Our cook packs our lunch in a tiffin box. Now it is time to dress up in my two pieces of 'business swami' ochre *dhoties.* I complete the 'look' with my modern design titanium glasses that guarantee the serious look required for a CEO. I add the final touches, which are the Rudraksha and other crystal bead *malas* around my neck. I am ready for my day at work.

Upon our arrival, the security guard gives us a military-style salute, clicks his heels together, and pushes his chin up. I feel odd to receive this mark of respect, but it seems it is the traditional way security personnel show respect. I would prefer a simple 'Good morning, Sir,' and a smile.

As I enter our premises, I first turn to the little temple in the lush tropical garden with frangipanis and bougainvilleas of all colours. I pay my respects to Lord Shiva, Lakshmi, Saraswathi, and of course, Lord Ganesh, the son of Lord Shiva.

He is the God with an elephant head and is always present to facilitate life. In India, you will see him everywhere — in every home, every office, factory, and in every temple. He will be honoured before laying the foundation of a house, before moving into a new home, before any new important action. He is easy to please. He is jovial and benevolent. Lord Shiva is the All, the All Pervading. He is ALL. Lakshmi, the wife of Vishnu is the one to bring prosperity and wealth, while Saraswathi takes care of our creativity — the power of work and beauty. Every Friday, we all assemble here for a *puja*, a ceremony to honour our deities, only attended by those who wish to. We do not impose on anybody to attend, as I strongly support the freedom of religious belief. I truly believe in tolerance in all its forms and that is what India is all about — tolerance, even though it may sometimes appear to not be so. Amongst our staff, we have a majority of Hindus, but there are also Christians, Muslims, and Agnostics too.

It is a short *puja*, bells are rung, incense is offered, the *deepam* is lit and the flame is moved in a clock-wise manner in front of the idols. We distribute kumkum (red powder that is placed like a dot on the forehead), *sandanam* (sandalwood powder) and ash. We distribute *prasadam* (an offering of food that has been given to the deities) to everyone. It concludes a week of work and leads to the weekend to be followed by a new week. This *puja* not only thanks God, in the form of all those deities, for whatever good He has given us, but also requests Him to ensure that good days come our way. I like this *puja* in our company as it brings everyone together and shows everyone that we have a common goal. It unifies the teams.

I am not a person to follow rituals, but there are many in our staff who are, hence I insist that we perform the *puja* without fail, every week. I do not condemn rituals and I feel that it is an important part of all religions. It allows people to feel close to the Ultimate.

Life is so hard for many people, we often have no listening shoulder to rest our heads on and cry silently. Seeing the statue of our favourite deity has a soothing effect on some people and helps us to continue our life despite our hardships. It even helps us overcome our hardship. Here is Lord Shiva, or Lord Ganesh, listening benevolently and kindly. Listening to our hearts, our cries, our demands and supplications. The priest with his chants calls for God's attention to our miseries and we can then continue our life, go home to our loneliness, or to our families with a softer heart. This is true for every religion. Like many Hindus, I prefer the quietness of my little *puja* room in my residence, or of our Shiva temple in our hermitage in Kolli Hills. However, I truly believe that one does not need to go to a temple to find God, to speak to God, or to feel God's presence. He/She/It is everywhere, and having this awareness deeply embedded in me, I do not feel that need to go looking for God. The same goes for having to perform the rituals at specific times, or at specific places.

This does not make sense to me as the Ultimate has not made any place better or worse than another. We make it so.

Nothing is either good, or bad for the Ultimate. For us a virus is bad, but for a virus, our antibodies are bad. Who says that a human is more important than a virus? A human is important for a virus to live. Without it, it dies. A virus cannot exist without a human, to live, procreate, and spread… same for the human race. We have no more or no less demands and capacities to adapt to a situation than a virus. They mutate as much as we have in the past millennia and still do, though at a much slower pace. Thus, for an Advaita Vedantic, there is nothing good and nothing bad.

I enter the main room where the cubicles are lined up in such a way as to form four sections, with an executive at its centre. Everyone stands up and wishes me a 'Good Morning' as I approach my own office. Pinky, my personal secretary, who has been looking after me for 14 years now, greets me too.

My computer-in-charge connects my laptop and ensures that everything is in order. I then rapidly go through the headlines of the various business newspapers and underline articles that are significant and give them to Jayapalan to go through. Pinky comes in, and informs me of the appointments for the day, while Vasan, our HR manager informs me of the situation regarding the employees present.

Pinky, like most of my employees has been with us for a long time. She is quite a surprising person, sharp and clever. She has very persuasive good manners and is hard-working. She actually has a diploma in aeronautical engineering and is an athlete, a sprinting champion for the state of Meghalaya where she comes from. She was the only girl in her year at the University of Madras for Aeronautics. She worked as an aeronautical engineer at Chennai Airport for a while, but in a male-dominated field, they were not particularly accomodating towards a woman.

The job sometimes called for night duties, which was definitely not the ideal situation for a woman in India. She gave her career up when her boss insisted that she only report for night duty. After a couple of years of working for an exporter, where I met her, she came to our company asking for the job of a secretary. I gave her the post, which she still occupies.

Of course, when she met me at first, she was shocked to see a swami heading the company, and that too a French man. After reading her CV, I told her, 'I do not need an aeronautical engineer. I need a personal secretary. Do you know how to use a PC?'

'No,' she answered, 'but I will learn fast.'

I enrolled her immediately. She is a great assistant for me as she is strong willed, will not let people take her for a ride and she works hard to make sure she gets what is needed for our company and myself. I can say she is devoted to me.

She is certainly very good in keeping our customers happy, and always manages to develop a nice friendship with them. Thanks to her, our customers always feel they are coming back home when they visit us. One interesting facet of her personality is that she is very devoted to Lord Shiva and that is important to me.

While Pinky is here in my office with a pile of cheques to sign, a quality controller is there in her office facing mine, while my French customer is sitting on an armchair in my corner seating arrangement. He looks completely lost seeing a swami dressed in flowing ochre robes. He must be wondering, 'What the heck is this swami doing here?'

I do not have much time to elaborate and tell him quickly, 'I am a Hindu monk... do not worry. After the initial shock, you will feel better later...' I am short of time, as usual, Jayapalan has arrived and we need to talk about an important matter.

It is already 34 years since we met in 1975. In these years, he has become my friend, my son, and my partner. He comes from a modest family of goldsmiths. He came to me during the days I had started Fabratel. I was all alone, with my divorce still fresh in my heart. We became friends immediately. I employed him immediately and put him in charge of our warehouse. Little by little I taught him everything I knew about fabric, garments, and everything about our business. After five years, we had become very close friends and after more than 30 years, there has never been one instance of financial problems between us.

Jayapalan had also been a witness to my spiritual quest. I am very thankful to him and his family for the support and respect he has always given me. Thanks to him, I met Raji, the Brahmin lady who brought me to Hinduism. He was a great support when I stopped smoking, as this was not acceptable to my Order. Smoking 60 cigarettes per day is a habit very difficult to get rid of and because of that I became extremely irritable. I must say I was impossible to deal with during those months, but Jayapalan was patient and understanding.

Jayapal has two children and he is very much a part of my family, as I am part of his. When my younger brother Gerard passed away, he was waiting for me at the arrival hall of the Delhi domestic airport. I was returning from Varanasi and on my way to France for his funeral. He had decided to come along with me to help me go through this tough moment in my life. I appreciate his kindness, tolerance, and honesty towards me — all of which are typical Indian qualities. If one day he decides to throw me out of his house, I will have to leave as I don't even have a tenant contract with him. He also owns the company's premises, a property that has gained very high value thanks to the IT industry boom in India. If he wanted to, he could just sell it and live all his life without ever having to work. He is also the administrator of our Ashram's Trust.

Though no one is indispensable, I have difficulty calling it a day, and go to my hermitage in Kolli Hills. It is true that I love my work and although I should get rid of my pride, I still have that urge in me to go on. I do not want our business, for which my mother sacrificed her savings, for which my younger brother gave me his unflinching support, to go to waste. Besides that, I do enjoy my work. I would find it difficult to do nothing and simply sit in our hermitage, withering away until my last breath.

I am looking for someone who will be the CEO of our establishment. He will have to take over most of my responsibilities soon, while I will remain the chairman. I will visit our office from time to time while he will run the company along with Jayapalan. I have the choice of taking someone from amongst our group of executives. I have my eyes on one of them who seems to fit the requirements. I have already given him some of the responsibilities.

These being the basics of any business, I have to entrust this high post to someone who is capable of following up with what is happening on the financial side of the business. Another possibility would be to find an appropriate person by looking outside our business, but I would prefer to work with someone who has been working with me for many years.

It is lunchtime for all of us and Jayapal and I go to our cafeteria where everyone has assembled in shifts, as it would not contain all the 80 people in our head office simultaneously. After the meal, we all enjoy a nice cup of steaming hermitage coffee. We relax a bit before going back to work, while some of the employees go out to smoke a cigarette. I do not allow anyone to smoke within the premises of our office. Only a few smoke and they don't smoke much either. In South India, it is considered bad manners to smoke in front of an elder, or the boss.

If I go out and talk to someone smoking in the street, he will hide his cigarette and talk to me as a gesture of respect towards a swami and an elder.

Back in my office, I am waiting to meet my banker regarding a loan we need. She is supposed to meet me at 2 p.m. and I am sure she will be late. All employees of nationalised banks here have a bad habit of being late for everything. They are Indian civil servants and act like kings. They are arrogant and wilfully confuse their customers with their never-ending paper work, and ask for the same information several times on different forms. Last year, my chartered accountant advised me to buy a new car for tax purposes and I chose a Skoda, as it would be ideal to pick up our customers and take them around in. Though we had enough funds to buy it, I applied for a loan. My banker, knowing our account performance with them, immediately gave us the go-ahead.

I ordered the car and just before it was to be delivered, my accountant told me that the bank had called to say that I would not be able to receive the loan for the purchase of the car, as '...the Reserve Bank of India does not permit banks to give loans to foreigners...'. I was furious as we had to go to our hermitage the next day and we had sold the previous car. Therefore, we would have to pay for the new car in cash just when our cash flow was tight.

I called my chartered accountant urgently and explained the problem. He confirmed that according to the Reserve Bank of India a foreign resident could indeed not receive a loan for buying a car or anything else for that matter. I asked Pinky to find out what the minimum balance would be to keep the account active and to immediately draw out all the funds from that account, save the minimum. The moment this was done, the bank manager called me up straight away and I explained to her in very strong words, my feelings regarding their behaviour and that she was wrong to refuse my loan. Within 30 minutes, she was at our reception, asking to meet me.

Pinky received her and brought her to me. In my office, she gave me a sheepish look while I looked angry. My Guru had taught me to feel 'anger without anger'. I am known for my sudden bouts of 'anger' when I see someone going too far, who needs to be stopped with a shaking up to bring him/her back onto the right track. They call me 'the volcano', but they do know that I never hold a grudge against anyone and I immediately forgive, but do not forget. I told the banker, 'You take advantage of the apparent naivety of your customers and you excel in making our lives more complicated by coming up with rules that do not exist. People show their confidence in you by entrusting you with safeguarding their hard-earned money. What are you doing with that? You use our money to make profit for your banks, and more, and more profit. I have decided to stop working with your bank.'

The banker was shaky and visibly embarrassed, 'Tell me how can I make amends for this unfortunate mistake on our part?'

'You give us the loan without interest.'

She suddenly became pale and asked me for two days of reflection.

A few hours later, probably after having consulted with her boss and their head office, she came back and said that they would give me the loan and I would have to pay interest, but at an incredibly low rate. I grabbed the offer and reverted the withdrawal of all my funds from that bank.

It does happen sometimes that anger threatens to overtake me... especially when there is an obvious lack of rigour in someone's work. Here in Tamil Nadu, they have a phrase they use regularly and it irritates me very much — '*Parwa ille*', which could be translated, as 'it is okay, but not up to the mark'. They say the same thing in Hindi — '*Chaltha Hai*'. This is extensively used in India and shows how little some workers care about a job well done.

However, I chant *Aum Namah Shivaya*, get a hold of myself and explain for the thousandth time why it is important that one should not be satisfied with *Parwa ille* or *Chaltha Hai*.

Benhur, a Catholic Christian born in Madras, is at the entrance of my office and asks me if he can come in and talk to me. I remember when I employed him, he had a Masters degree in mathematics. I took him in immediately and he wanted to start the very moment I accepted him. He agreed to a ridiculously low salary of Rs. 500 for being quality controller. He had to go to factories from morning to evening to check the quality of the products we had ordered from exporters. Those were hard days for him as he had to spend long hours in hot, dusty, noisy factories, trying to find out what was wrong with the products the exporters were manufacturing and imposing the clients' views on them; all that with a smile and being polite. He has married a Brahmin woman and they now have a bright little boy they are very proud of.

I am proud of Benhur. He comes from time to time to see me in my office, seeking advice related to his work, or even spiritual doubts. Today, he deals with more than one million pieces per year and handles prestigious accounts. Benhur is one of the best-paid employees in our company and I see in him the material of a possible future CEO. I know that he could handle this provided he learns a few more tricks of the trade. We now have branch offices in Bengaluru, Tirupur, and a liaison office in Delhi. We also have a representative in France who covers Europe.

At 9 p.m., we go home. I am exhausted and my legs are heavy. My varicose veins are troubling me. Road traffic is incredibly messy at this time and it will take us 45 minutes to reach home. Arriving home at last, I remove my two pieces of clothing and I am again the naked Naga Swami. I rush to the bathroom and take a welcome shower as today we have had lots of power failures, as is usual in the hottest days of summer, I feel sweaty and sticky.

Our cook is here to give us our dinner. After eating, I open my laptop and start chatting with my disciples from all over the world. I have Sunny online from our ashram telling me they had 46 mm of rain last night. Our dry well has filled up at the right time and the coffee plantation looks better every day. My personal assistant and I take our dinner on a mat on the floor as always.

Before retiring to sleep, it is close to midnight, I am thinking and ask myself as I do often, why should I not leave all this and run to our hermitage and live peacefully in the silence of the surrounding hills and forest. Nevertheless, I remember what my Guruji told me, 'You have to bring spirituality in the material life.'

38

KARMA

The most important thing I have learnt is to live from day to day as though there will be no tomorrow. Since tomorrows are made of todays, it is enough to live today in the best way possible, without thinking about tomorrow. Of course, other parameters have to be taken into account. For example, good actions have to be done during the 'now' so that the tomorrows will bring us good Karma. This is the very principle of Karma — we are entirely responsible for what we do, all the actions we take, or *not*. Here is the issue and the difficult part of it — it is precisely what we ought not to do that will create painful tomorrows. When I talk about actions, I do not mean only the visible physical actions, but also mental ones. As the *Bhagavad Gita* says, 'Do the actions without thinking about its resulting effects, as they are bound to come'. In the actions/ reactions process, we can only be in control of the first one, the action (mental or physical).

Let us take for example the action-reaction scenario when one throws a ball against a wall.

We can decide what ball, when, where, and how to throw the ball. The results however, are not entirely in our control. That part is controlled by the Ultimate. Since we cannot entirely control that and the Ultimate's decisions are not known to us, even if the astrologers and other soothsayers claim the opposite for a fee, why bother about it?

Let us concentrate on the now so that we have a good later. Furthermore, why bother about the past and cry over it? Isn't it better to take lessons from what has happened and try not to repeat painful mistakes?

I live my today, my now, fully. When I am in our hermitage, as I prefer to call our ashram, I like to find myself again, to get back on track to fulfilment, to reunite with my Self, with Nature, with the Ultimate. I enjoy the instant so fully, so immensely.

There, surrounded by tall silver oak trees, I often sit and look around me and see myself in everything surrounding me. I feel one with it — with the flowers of all hues and scents, bees of all kinds buzzing from one flower to another, with the trees of so many green shades moving gently in the breeze and clouds of all shapes, softly brushing the top of the hills around me. I feel it in all kinds of birds twittering in the hibiscus bushes, the ants of all colours and shapes hurrying in their lines of duty, the squirrels with their staccato sharp little screams as though emphasising each panache-filled movement of their fluffy striped tails, and in the aroma of the *agharbattis* burning in our temple after my morning *sadhana*. I feel one with the gentle wind taking possession of all around and myself. I am One. I am All That Is.

In my Madras office, all my energy, all my concentration, all my attention goes into the running of Fashions International, now renamed Christian Fabre Textiles Pvt. Ltd. How to function better, to find new customers, to face the global financial turmoil that followed the Kuwait war, September 11, 2001, and the 2008-09 recession. I have to make sure our company not only survives all these difficult times, but progresses even further.

Karma will be the result of my choice of actions. Actions done or not done but only thought of. If I do not sow, I will not be able to reap the fruits. A Chinese proverb says, 'The best time to plant a tree was twenty years ago. The next best time is now.' This is what Karma is all about and this is how I lead my life.

One should always introspect, however. What have I done to get this result, whether it is on a physical or an intellectual level? There is no need to cry for myself, as it won't change anything about the situation I am in now. Instead, it is better to think, to meditate, on how I can change the present by finding out what I did wrong in the past, and why and when I did it wrong, so that I can rectify it by acting now with a positive productive result. To feel guilty about the bad result of one's bad action is counterproductive. Instead, it is better to immediately act in a good manner to counter balance the bad action, with a smile...

Those rules of life could appear to be simplistic, but try to follow them and you will understand how much hardship they will create for you. But then, what peace one gets!

To be in the present moment, to not regret the past, to not project oneself into the future, but instead, to build the moment, the Now... this is what one has to remember.

Never take Life too seriously. Laugh heartily. Do not pay too much importance to anything that does not deserve it. Do not analyse yourself all the time. It could bring you more harm than good. Some *shishyas* say, 'I did wrong...'. Or, 'I have done nothing about it...'

To which I answer, 'Ok, you did it. It's over. What is done cannot be undone.'

Moreover, I add, 'It is not *That* who acted, it is your physical self who did it, it is your body who committed the mistake. You are not the body; you are not the physical self. Only you, the Self, the Ultimate will remain when your body and mind dissolve.'

To torture one's mind does not bring any positive result, but is the natural reaction of most Westerners according to their Christian/Semitic cultural upbringing, where the idea of mistake, of sin, is met with the terrible threat of a vengeful God, who will punish us for those bad actions. This idea of sin is alien to those who believe the Advaita Vedanta.

A God who punishes? Nothing is further from the truth than this idea. We punish ourselves by the bad actions we commit and no one else. God is neither kind nor terrible. *He is*, that is all. My Guruji used to tell me, 'Just *be*.'

Many people believe in chance or luck. There is no such thing. It is your actions that will translate into reactions. The reactions will come to you as and when, in this instant or later in your next incarnation, the Ultimate decides. The popular wisdom that says, 'Men propose and God disposes', is absolutely true. It is Karma.

What is the most important to know, then to feel, and then to be conscious of in every moment, is that we are the Shiva, the Ultimate. What, or Who, makes our body, this machine that we are, tick? What or Who makes this Universe what it is?

Then, when we can feel that nothing is higher or lower than us, nothing is more or less important than us, that nothing is ugly or pretty, that nothing is tall or small, then we are very close to the Realisation that we are That, we are Shiva, because we are not this body. This is the reason why saints such as Ramana Maharshi or Paramahamsa Ramakrishna accepted the cancer that was eating them up, as part of the Self and did not perceive it to be a God-sent revenge or punishment.

They also knew that their cancer is the reaction of their past actions from a previous life, and they accepted this as fact.

I know that death is terrible. I suffered a lot when first my father, then my elder brother, my young nephew, my younger brother, and finally my mother died. I suffered even more watching helplessly when my mother was in the grip of Alzheimer's disease. Dead bodies are like machines that have stopped functioning. The Self, however, is ever present in the atoms in the shape of these bodies. When the body/machine stops, the atoms and energy reshape themselves into other entities, be it the sky, the earth, the birds, the air, the clouds, the space... as there is nothing and nowhere where *It is not.* 'It' being the Ultimate Consciousness.

Of course, Karma is an acceptable fact only if one also accepts the principle of reincarnation. However, one can easily understand and accept the concept that atoms, or rather energy, cannot disappear. It transforms itself into other entities.

When at last I understood the notion of Karma, it was like watching a jigsaw puzzle solve itself. Once we discover the concept, everything fits perfectly. Then the angle of our Life's vision changes radically. I understood the whys of everything. It is like when we see someone chain-smoking all day. We know he is preparing a horrible death for himself, that he may not be aware of. Does he know when he is 20 years old that smoking will bring death to him? I don't think so. Everyone thinks it is someone else who will die and not he. He thinks he will escape, but his Karma will catch up with him much later.

It has also changed me. It makes me see my life from a different perspective, from a different viewpoint and angle, with more lenience towards myself and everything else that forms part of our world.

Accepting myself as I am, without trying to find escape, to see myself clearly as I am, not judging myself, made me love myself and love everything else around me, my family, my friends, unknown people, acquaintances, and people on the street. I learned how not to hate as I learned to be compassionate and care for others by being so with myself. I am made the way I am. I did not make myself the way I am.

Those genes were given to me by my parents, not only thanks to their act of procreation, but also because of the Karmas that enjoined them to act in what resulted in Who and What I am today. Love makes the whole difference. Once we 'Realise' that, Love makes us feel One with All. When one loves oneself, one forms a whole with everybody and then Love for oneself automatically becomes Love for everyone.

Love is so important. Unfortunately, the word has been used and misused in all kinds of contexts and not always in the best way. It has since then lost its powerful meaning. Love is respect for one another and the ability to give without expecting anything in return. It is also accepting others the way they are. It is not only tolerance, but also acceptance.

We have to be sure we do not love *mainly* or *only* ourselves. Sometimes it only takes a crisis with a woman, man, friend, parent, or a husband for that love to evaporate. Some couples separate from each other after having loved each other passionately. They become enemies driven by hate to the point of tearing each other apart. Is that love? Do you sincerely believe that God has ceased to love you just because you have erred on the wrong side of the path? Equally, do you really think that God hates you because you have gone astray from the path of righteousness?

One has to make lots of effort to love and be good of course, especially with those who are not very nice to you. It certainly is easier to be bad, rough, and arrogant. In Chennai, when I come back to my residence exhausted after 10-12 hours of work, after spending the whole day solving exasperating issues, and someone knocks at my door or pops up online wanting to chat with me, frankly speaking, I feel like telling him to go and get lost and leave me in peace, but I make an effort to get myself interested in his/her problem. What if that person needs a helping hand at that precise moment? One kind word, one smile, a little word of love to him or her could make his or her life easier to bear. After this, it is up to him or her to receive my offer of love or not.

The first two qualities I am asking from my disciples are humility and compassion. I always try to give them the instrument that will allow them to become better people, to open one's eyes and to become conscious.

I am very often asked, 'Why are you a Hindu? Why did you give up the religion of your ancestors? Have you retained any part of Western culture?' I tell them, 'I am not a Christian and I am not a Hindu. The good words that Christ preached to his disciples and all those who wanted to hear, are for me as important as the words in the *Avadhuta Gita*.'

A certain rigour remains in me from my origins, my sense of discipline, and my civic sense, which is unfortunately lacking in India. Maybe I have also inherited the love of things well made. I certainly have retained my critical faculties and have made my motto — 'Without the freedom to criticise there is no flattering praise,' as written by Pierre-Augustin Caron de Beaumarchais, a French playwright in the 18th century.

I have always believed this and I use it in my teachings. The most important part of the teachings of Christianity that has remained in me mainly refers to Love for others.

Love one another.

— John 8:34

This message was a revolutionary statement more than 2000 years ago and it still is today.

I found this in Hinduism:

The other is you.

I am neither a Hindu, nor a Christian, but simply a human being who tries hard to be a better one Now, not better than someone else, but better than what I was a moment ago.

I am often asked what has changed in me during the last 30 years. Come on look at me! What a question! Inside I am not the same person. Christian Fabre is so far away that when someone calls me by that name I do not react immediately, especially when it is in India where everyone knows me as Swamiji. I have the impression that someone else is being called out.

What remains of this Christian is only the feeling that he has lost a lot of time.

I do notice that deep inside me, there still remains a fundamental impatience, a need to make everything move fast. Slow, lazy people, the could-not-care-less ones annoy me. I must work hard on myself to lessen this negative trait. Also, my anger surfaces from time to time, up from my throat and chokes me, especially when I am tired and facing a bad situation, or when someone does something bad. I control it or rather, do my best to control it. The ones who joined me in the early days of our company still remember my terrible fits of anger and my nickname 'The Volcano'. Although they still call me that I control my anger so much that I might just come to a point of terrible eruption.

I try hard not to hurt anyone and never use swear words. Nowadays, I have mastered the art of pretending to be angry to such a point that they do not know whether I am truly angry or I am faking it.

It is essential to convey the feeling that the boss is thoroughly 'pissed off' by your way of working, your attitude, or something unproductive. It is important not to hurt the feelings of anyone. Tamil people are a proud and sensitive cultured race and one has to be careful how the truth is conveyed. Some truths are not always good to tell. I never hated anyone, not even my wife when we separated. I always forgive, but I never forget. Hate is a word that has no meaning for me.

39

IN MEDITATION TILL THE END OF TIME

How will I be another 10 or 15 years from now? I can tell you how I feel about it. Some people thought that a community of people, men and women living a harmonious life, would surround me. I do not know if that will happen. Maybe that is how I will be and maybe that is not what I will be. It does not depend on me. I leave it to the Ultimate to decide which Karma He will send me. I have no way of influencing this decision. So, why worry about it? Surely, I know what my aim is. It is to widen the circle of those who will be touched by what I am trying to convey through this book, those who will know a little more of what Hinduism is about and share a bit of the India I fell in love with. We cannot dissociate Hinduism from India. Ask any Hindu and he will tell you that Hinduism is not a religion. He will tell you that it is a way of life and for each person it shows how one can lead every moment as closely aligned as possible to the Ultimate Reality.

The religion that is being practised in India has in fact, no name. The ancient people of India used to call it Sanatana Dharma, the eternal teaching. It seems the Portuguese called it Hinduism. Long ago, Hindus and Christians were called Hindus because they lived along the river Indus.

Hindus have suffered a lot from successive Muslim invasions, but fortunately, there were also good Muslim rulers who were enlightened and adapted themselves to the Hindu way of life and were very good for India.

Like Christians praying to the statues of Saints, Hindus also pray to Divinities, representing different aspects of the Ultimate. Hinduism is not a religion and does not expect people to pray to millions of Gods. It is only because of the various representations of particular aspects of Brahman (The Ultimate Consciousness), that Westerners mistake Hinduism to be polytheistic, whereas it is very much a monotheistic belief. It is not a blind belief. It is a strong conviction generated by a deep consciousness that we are All One. An anthropomorphic representation of one aspect of Brahman, as for example Lord Shiva, facilitates a relationship and allows a simple communication with the Ultimate in the shape of a personal God. Once the mind of the believer raises questions as to who is Lord Shiva, who is this, who is that, then comes the understanding in the mind that it is only this statue representing Lord Shiva to which I am praying, or talking to. It is a catalyst, which will enable me to communicate with the Ultimate by a transfer of Energy from me to It.

Despite the imposition of Catholicism in Europe, sometimes in a very horrific manner (read about the Inquisition that raged in the dark years of the Middle Ages in Europe), ancient beliefs of the Gallic tribes are as widely followed now, as they have been absorbed by the French Catholics. Catholics of today are not very different from their simple Hindu counterparts.

The French Catholics pray to St. Christopher to make sure their journey is trouble free, whereas the Hindus pray to Lord Ganesh to ensure that the day will go smoothly. I can directly 'synchronise' with the Self at any moment, whereas people who have not had the opportunity to understand this will need to pray to the Divinity of their liking and humbly request them to take away whatever troubles they are facing in their daily life. Only the words change, the way of doing it changes, but the aim is the same. There is however, a great difference between spirituality and religion.

I cannot say I am a religious man, but I am definitely a spiritual man. A religious man will be required to go through a series of rituals, whereas I do not. If I ever do it is always in the form of *japa* (a repetition of a name of the Ultimate, or a mantra). As I need only to connect with the Self, which is All, which is everywhere at all times, there is no place where It is not, no time when It is not.

I do not know if the Western world accepts differences. I do not think so, even though it calls itself 'developed'. We need only to open an international magazine where there are plenty of examples of how barbaric some Western 'developed' nations are. In India, despite all the taboos related to the caste system, there are so many religions practised here and a greater tolerance. St. Thomas was warmly welcomed here when he sought refuge in Kerala when Jerusalem was plundered. The Jews found refuge in this country, which is the only one to have never persecuted them until now. The Parsis, the great followers of Zoroaster, were welcomed and were able to settle and thrive in this country and are today very much a part of the great development that can be witnessed in Indian industry and the army. Tibetans were allowed to settle here when the Chinese invaded their country and they are allowed to follow their own culture and government in the north of India.

Coming to India, one has to leave behind all his/her preconceived notions and my advice for everyone who reads this book, is see yourself in others, because the others are you. I know, it is difficult to see oneself in a beggar who comes and knocks on your car window... he is nothing less than you. The grumpy ticket collector in the bus who might give you a well-meaning, dazzling smile someday, the mad cap drivers, and there are so many in this country, who nearly engineer accidents because they do not bother to check if they are endangering someone… they are also You, your Self.

In about three years, I shall be 70 years old. The French government has granted me my retirement pension by allotting me a royal 367 Euros per month! I know, it's a pittance and totally inadequate for living in Europe, but I welcome this, as it is enough for me to live on when I leave our company and retire fully to live in our hermitage/ ashram.

I must admit that I enjoy working in our company. I enjoy working with our team of young people. I am aware that I will have to re-structure our company so that I can at last, devote more time to myself, to apply the brakes, to slow down, and spend more time in Kolli Hills. I sincerely wish to find someone who will take over. Someone to whom I could say, 'Here are the reigns of my chariot. Please drive it carefully and surely.' Maybe I will also travel around the world giving lectures to those who invite me. I have done that several times already, in as far-off places as Sao Paulo and even in France. Do I fear death? I do not fear it in this instant. How I will feel when it comes to me, I do not know.

Hopefully, I will be allowed, like my father, to go softly, silently away, but it cannot be my choice. The Ultimate, Lord Shiva, will decide. After all death is life and life is death. It is a complete circle. The shape of the Shiva Lingam expresses this never-ending cycle of life and death. Therefore, death is not a defeat. It is not the end of all. Hindus believe it is a privilege to be born a human being, to have been allowed to incarnate on this planet as a human being. The Ultimate has given us a brain to think and feel emotions, to reason, to hate or love, which will allow us to 'realise' our Self. We are the only creatures, who have been given so much. Why then pray to the Ultimate when It has given you so much? Why ask for more when we have everything?

The Experience I went through while visiting and meditating in the Lord Shiva Temple of Vriduchallam was not a vision of the moment, but rather a continuous experience, which I still re-live very often, every day, except when I am exhausted. I am still in the same spiritual condition today, as I was in 1988 despite the numerous problems I had to go through. Of course, dark clouds and storms have often shadowed that great moment of peace, but my Consciousness is always with me in all circumstances.

Meanwhile situations, difficult to find solutions for, have come up. Nevertheless, the Ultimate has not only sent me bad Karmas of hardship, it has also sent me good ones and even very good ones. I am now at peace with myself, together with John, my companion, who the Ultimate has sent to help me reach my end peacefully and gracefully. Despite my age, I still feel the need to be of use to someone. Age, however, imposes constraints on my body. I cannot do things I used to do 21 years ago and I enjoy teaching John as if he was my son, how to improve himself and be a successful man. My bones and joints ache, my blood circulation is a bit disrupted and I cannot run up the road of our hermitage because of my varicose veins. Crying over my problems will not bring any solution as I have learnt so many years ago and as Swami Sarveswara, my beloved Guruji has taught me, 'Everything is mortal, even a stone, except the Self.'

What is the advice I could give to people?

Anyone can follow this path. You alone can take the

decision to take this path and follow it. I can show you the direction, but the decision to stay on the path can rest only in you, and not in your Guru. You cannot blame him if you take another direction and do not achieve any results and come back more confused.

Am I a preacher? Not at all. As I have said, I am simply a human being, with a little knowledge.

It is true that I would like my remains to stay in India. Then again, what would I feel if my bones are resting elsewhere? Will it make a difference to my Self? No, no difference at all.

In India, swamis are never burnt like most Hindus. They are buried, as it is believed that a swami's body continues to radiate the aura he had during his lifetime. If this is done, I would love it to be near my cypress trees in our Hermitage in Kolli Hills, and I should be seated in the Padmasana (lotus position) so that I will be able to continue my meditation till the end of time.

GLOSSARY

Advaita	Non-duality. There is no duality between the subject that knows and an object that is known. No object is ever known apart from the subject that knows it. So, in truth they are not two, but only one.
Agharbatthis	Incense sticks
Ahimsa	Non-violence as taught by Mahatma Gandhi.
Ashram	Spiritual retreat. Place for meditation and spiritual growth, usually centred around the teachings of a Guru.
Aurobindo	(1872-1950) Indian nationalist, poet, philosopher, and yogi.
Autorickshaws	Yellow and black three-wheel motorbike taxis.
Avadhuta	Somewhat eccentric type of mystic or saint who has risen above body-consciousness, duality, and worldly

concerns and acts without consideration of standard social etiquette. Such personalities are considered to be free from ego and to 'roam free like children' over the face of the earth. An Avadhuta does not identify with the body or mind.

Bharat — Ancient name of India

Bidi — Cheap Indian handmade cigarettes

Bhagavad Gita — One of the major scriptures of Hinduism. Officially part of the epic *Mahabharata*. Teaches different paths so that one may be in union with God (or liberation).

Bhajans — Devotional Hindu songs

Bhakti — Devotion to God

Bindu — Little point or dot. Devotional/mystical dot applied to forehead in Hinduism.

Bollywood — The Hollywood of Mumbai

Brahman — Eternal, omnipotent, omniscient, omnipresent, impersonal Reality of all beings and everything else in this Universe.

Brahmin — Class of educators, law makers, scholars, and preachers in Hinduism.

Caste System — Assignment of individuals to places in the social hierarchy determined by cultural heritage.

Cartesian — Relating to French philosopher and mathematician Renée Descartes.

CEO	Chief Executive Officer
Chakra	Nerve plexuses or centres along the spine and in the head through which the Kundalini energy is led.
Chappati	North Indian round roasted bread
Dal	Lentil-based stew eaten with rice and/or chapattis
Dharma	Religious term that means one's righteous duty or virtuous path. Law of higher truth.
Dhuny	Sacred fire
Diksha	Ritual of Initiation
Ganesh	Shiva's son with the head of an elephant. The remover of obstacles.
Ganja	Marijuana
Guru	Lit. 'dispeller of darkness'. A spiritual teacher who has realised the Self and who is able to use his or her power to assist others in attaining the goal of Self-realisation.
Hatha yoga	Preparatory stage of physical purification that the body practises for higher meditation.
Idli	Steamed rice cakes
Japa	Lit. muttering or whispering. A muttered prayer consisting of reciting and repeating

	passages from scriptures, mantras, or names of a deity as a means of stilling the mind and invoking grace.
Gnana	True Knowledge
Karma	The effects of a person's past actions on his or her present and future state. Principle of causality. The law of retributive action.
J. Krishnamurthi	(1895-1986) Renowned writer and speaker on philosophical and spiritual subjects. Raised under the tutelage of Annie Besant of the Theosophical Society.
Kundalini	A form of yoga practised in India, primarily in the school of Tantra. The term means serpent power, the energy which is believed to lie dormant in the human being and which through breath control and other means is made to travel through various *chakras* along the spine to be ultimately united with universal energy located on the top of the head. The deliberate rousing of the Kundalini can be dangerous.
Kurta	Indian-style, long-sleeved shirt worn loosely over pajama-style pants.
Lingam	Lit. mark or sign. Symbol for the worship of Shiva.

Mala	Rosary of 108 beads used in the practice of *japa*, also garland
Mantra	A series of syllables, considered sacred, used in meditation and rituals. One of the most common forms of *sadhana*.
Maya	Cosmic illusion where one appears as many. The misconception whereby the ephemeral world of appearances is taken to be real.
Nisargadatta Maharaj	(1897-1981) The most famous Advaita teacher since Ramana. The bidi-seller from Mumbai's book, *I am That*, is still widely studied today.
OM/Aum	The primordial sound from which all creation springs. It is the most important element in many mantras.
Padmasana	Asana means position. Lotus position, to encourage breathing and physical stability for meditative practice.
Pradakshina	The practice of circumambulation in a clockwise direction, around a person or holy object as an act of veneration.
Pranam	Salutation
Pranayama	Control of the life force by practising breath control.
Prasadam	Sacred offering to the deity returned to the devotee after the worship as part of the deity's grace

Puja	Devotional ritual and prayer
Pujari	Priest performing the puja
Rajas	The three operating principles known as *gunas*. No single *guna* can exist without the other two. *Rajas* pertains to motion, energy, activity or excitability.
Rajiv Gandhi	(1944-1991) Elder son of Indira Gandhi, who became Prime Minister of India for four years, after her death.
Sri Ramakrishna	(1836-1886) Represents the very core of spiritual realisations of the seers and sages of India. His whole life was literally an uninterrupted contemplation of God.
Ramana Maharshi	(1879-1950) Attained liberation at the age of 16 and spent the rest of his life at the sacred mountain Arunachala. Although his strongest transmission was through silence, his method of self-inquiry through the question 'Who am I', was the first teaching of Advaita to cross over to Western culture.
Ravi Shankar	(1920—) Famous Indian sitar player and composer.
Rudraksha	The Rudraksha seed is sacred to Shiva. He is usually depicted wearing a necklace of these seeds and many Shiva devotees use them as rosaries. They are worn around the neck to purify the body.

Sadhana	Spiritual practice. Traditional *sadhanas* are meditation (*dhyana*), inquiry (*jnana*), devotion (*bhakti*) and selfless service (*seva*). Different people are suited to different kinds of *sadhana*.
Sadhu	An ascetic solely dedicated to achieving *moksha* (liberation) through meditation and contemplation of Brahman.
Samadhi	Mausoleum of a saint. Also the term for an intensely blissful state of consciousness induced by complete meditation.
Sanskrit	The classical language of India in which most religious and spiritual literature was composed.
Sannyasin	Men or women who have 'renounced' the world; monks.
Sattvic	Endowed with a mellow, light and spiritual quality. One of the three governing *gunas* (principles).
Seva	Selfless work
Shankaracharya	The foremost exponent of Advaita (non-dualistic) Vedanta hailing from South India during 8th century A.D.
Shakti	Lord Shiva's consort, female energy
shanti	Peace.
shishya	Disciple.
Siddhi	Lit. perfection, accomplishment, success.

	Supernormal perceptual states, spiritual power or psychic ability, usually, as a result of intense *sadhana.*
Shlokas	Verses in Sanskrit texts; hymns of praise in Hindu scriptures.
Swami	A form of addressing spiritual teachers, or one's favourite deity.
Tamas	The operating principle of inactivity, laziness, inertia, dullness, or sloth.
Tapasaya/Tapas	Intense austerity exercises with the result of mastering body and mind.
Tiffin	Packed lunch
Trishul	Traditional Indian trident
Vedanta	A system of Hindu monotheistic ('All is God, God is All') philosophy founded on the *Upanishads* of the *Vedas.*
Yoga	Lit. joining or union. In general, a path of liberation. More specifically, the system of physical and mental discipline and meditation propounded by Patanjali.

TIMELINE

June 8, 1942	Born in Beziers
1944 (2 yrs)	Move to Cerbere
1946-1949 (4-7yrs)	Haemophilia
1949-1956 (7-14yrs)	Return to Beziers. Lakanal School
1957-1958 (15+16 yrs)	Lysee Henri IV
1959-1960	Private Commerce School
1960	Six months in England as an exchange student
1961-June 1963	Military Service
1963	Short vacation on a beach
Sept 1, 1963	SNCF (6 months)
1964 - 1970	Travel Agent. Met wife.
1966	Married, Nicolas born
Oct 26, 1971	Arrival in India
1973	Total Collapse
1974	Divorce

1974	Fabratel
1975	Met Jayapalan Shop in Taj
1983	Shivashakti Malabar Coast
1986	Met Guruji
Jan 26, 1988	Sannyas
1988	Fashions International
1989	Kenzo
1995	Bought Hermitage Land. Two years to complete
1998	Haridwar Maha Kumbh Mela
1999	Buy office land. One year to complete
1999	Swami Vedananda dies
	Jacques dies when Swami is in Paris
	Nephew dies
2001	Gerard dies. Swami at Allahabad Kumb Mela.
2005	Mom dies
Feb 2005	Guruji dies.
Oct 26, 2005	Dude started
June 8, 2008	Christian Fabre started

SUMMARY

1. You've Certainly Come a Long Way

I'm standing with my team on the top of Table Mountain in Africa. The breathtaking view makes my mind go back to Madras, many years ago, where I was starving, fighting against all odds.

2. My Super Shirts

My childhood memories about growing up in the south of France in a tight-knit, loving family. My father made fantastic toys with wood. He helped freedom fighters escape into Spain. I worked in my uncle's pastry bakery on Sundays. The family picked grapes in the season. My mother was a remarkable seamstress and made all our clothes. I have devout feelings, but my father forbids me from becoming a priest. I spend my carefree teenage years on the beaches.

3. Night of the Jackal

Military service. Training in Montelimar Barracks and since then, I remain a staunch anti-militarist. First experience of meditation in the 'hole'. 1961 in the Algerian War. One night on guard duty, I shoot an intruder, which turns out, to my relief, to be only a jackal.

4. A New Page

After an unhappy stint working for the French National Railways, I work as a travel agent, which allowed me to travel around the world. I get married and my son is born. I work as a real estate agent. One of my clients, who headed Kreglinger France, offers to train me and I am sent to Madras, in India, as a buyer of semi-tanned leather.

5. Shocking India

First impressions and working in India in the 1970s. Our curious and not-so-private life with our helpful servants. Perumal, my driver invites me for a meal at his modest home. Observations of India and her people.

6. Life is Cool

We have been in India for a year now. We move to an attractive colonial style house in a posh area and live the high-life of expatriates. I am a bit out of tune with Indian people and their culture. I take no interest in music or spirituality. I discover India through business trips. Travel to the Himalayas.

7. Rock Bottom

Everything collapses and I lose my job, house, and car. Can't face returning to France a failure and decide to stay in Madras. Think about designing and manufacturing garments in Madras for export to France, but the administrative work to set this up takes a long time. My wife leaves me and takes our son. I have no money. I feel suicidal.

8. A Little Frenchman in Madras

Meet a Parsi gentleman, who believes in my potential. We start a company called Fabratel. My mother sends money to buy the minimum equipment needed to start my own collection. Bluffing our way, we land a substantial order with a Parisian department store. I slave away and my partner gallivants in the Club. I design a line of men's shirts and sell it to the rich and famous in the Taj Coromandel hotel in Chennai. My mother comes to visit.

9. Shivashakti

I leave my Parsi partner and with Jayapal, I start the 'Shivashakti' company. I design and manufacture garments for a big store in Basel. We spent four months of the year in Switzerland. Despite a better financial situation, I head straight towards a nervous breakdown, by smoking and drinking too much. Then the Ultimate sends me a sign.

10. Raji Opens the Door

Raji, my neighbour, introduces me to Spirituality. I read *The Gospel Of Paramahamsa Ramakrishna*. Suddenly, I understand the treasure of India I had unknowingly been living close to for so many years. After reading the book, I understood that the reason to live is to get to know oneself. The Little Frenchman from Beziers feels a fever for Knowledge now. Get introduced to *bhajans*.

11. These Thoughts Are Not Yours

I end all bad habits, become a vegetarian and practise yoga. My teacher, Swami Vedananda, teaches me about Lord Shiva and how to meditate. It takes a year of meditation before I find that surprisingly my mind has quietened.

12. Malabar Coast

We stop our business in Switzerland and start our own brand of men's shirts to sell in multi-brand outlets in France. I make a collection of 20 shirts, we find a sales representative and soon we have an order of 20,000 pieces. My mother takes a mortgage on her house as collateral for a loan from a French bank. With loads of problems, we manufacture the order and ship the order on time. I deliver it myself. Our three main customers go bankrupt and I work very hard to get most of the stores to pay us. My mother gives me more of her savings. My friends take a personal loan to help me get back to India and think of something new.

13. Five Seconds for Eternity

Swami Vedananda takes me to meet his Guru, Swami Sarveswara. He suffers from leprosy and has lost his hands and feet. It was a mysterious meeting during which he tells me that I would soon see beyond the illusions around me and that I will become very famous. I experience an overwhelming wave of affection, and beauty.

14. You Are Shiva and Nothing Else

Every weekend, I undertake an arduous trip to be with

Swami Sarveswara. He makes a miracle happen one hot day. I marvel at how he can live with a mutilated body, and yet be happy, and calm. He talks to me about who and what Shiva is. My Guru tells me to go to a certain temple on a certain day.

15. My Life Changes

At the temple of Vriduchallam, I fall into a deep four-hour meditation and have an incredible vision of a Shiva Lingam surrounded by flames and covered with white flowers. From this moment onwards, my life changes.

16. He/She/It

My Guru, Swami Sarveswara, answers the questions that arose from the vision. Why did I experience a male and female presence?

17. Covered by the Four Winds

My Guru says that I am ready to take Sannyas Diksha. As preparation, he sends me to Varanasi for some rituals and on January 26, 1988, in a traditional ceremony, I am re-born as Swami Pranavananda Brahmendra Avadhuta. He instructs me to continue with my profession, as I will be able to help others and share with them what I have acquired through Lord Shiva. I am given a set of dhotis to wear in public and in private I am to be covered by the four winds as dictated by our lineage.

18. The Birth of Fashions International

We start a company to sell my knowledge of the garment

industry in India to international clients who would like to have their products manufactured here and exported to their countries. With modest beginnings, we work very hard, and soon make Chipie our customer. At the same time, I perform my daily *sadhana* and meditate every day.

19. The One Who Has Aum in His Heart

The most difficult, yet fullest period of my life begins. To renounce all, yet sign cheques of big amounts, to be naked next to men wrapped in their suits and ties. With only one exception, everybody at work has no problem accepting me as Swami. My Guru supports me through times of disappointment.

20. Being Monk and CEO

After my initiation, business starts to take off. Lee Cooper and Kenzo become customers. I buy an Ambassador car and then later a Maruti Suzuki. Go through tough times with the lady buyer from Chipie. After many failures, at last business succeeds.

21. Advaita

The meaning of Advaita, the philosophical system on which rests the foundation of my Order, is revealed to me. I learn about how to proceed to achieve the realisation of our real Self.

22. My Guru and His Lineage

Stories and anecdotes of some of the sages from my Guru's lineage — Sadashiva Brahmendra Avadhuta, Judge

Swamigal, and Swami Swayamprakash Brahmendra Avadhuta, also the little that I know of my Guru's life story.

23. You Will Build an Ashram

As instructed by my Guru, I start looking for a location to build an ashram. During weekends, after visiting my Guruji, I carry on with my spiritual practice in Thiruchengodu. There I see Kolli Hills in the distance.

24. Kolli Hills

Eventually, I find land for the ashram as instructed by my Guru. Doraiswami builds a mud house for us to live in.

25. Living in a Mud House

I meet Sunny and he comes to live on the land. He becomes the manager. He finds a building contractor and we start building the ashram.

26. White Swami with the Matchbox Car

After ten years of Fahions International we move to the new headquarters. I experience a nightmare trip in the rain to the ashram. Sunny marries Ruby and we run a small clinic at the ashram for the locals. After a horrible accident I buy a safer vehicle.

27. The Pink Strawberry in the Forest

My Guru stated long ago that I would be known all over the world. It starts with an article in a local Tamil magazine and this leads to more articles, and television programmes all over the world. My Guru falls ill with tuberculosis, which we could cure, but then he passed away from complications arising because of diabetes.

28. My Good-life Loving Family

My elder brother Jacques dies and my younger brother Gerard is diagnosed with cancer. I invite him to India. Gerard and his wife come again, and visit Varanasi. After they leave, I met the *ganja*-smoking Claus who comes to our ashram, and turns over a new leaf.

29. Maha Kumbh-Mela

I am accepted into the Juna Akhada and am able to attend the 1998 Maha Kumbh Mela in Haridwar. The highlight is the traditional bath, during which I am part of a procession of 100,000 naked men as they take a dip in the Ganga. Things get out of hand and we end up running for our lives.

30. Aum Shanti Shanti Shanti

I sing in the church during the funeral of my brother Gerard. My mother starts to lose her mind.

My sister-in-law takes care of her.

31. The Story of Dude

We started our own brand called Dude, and we were doing very well, when another company sued us and we had to stop.

32. Guru-disciple Relationship

This chapter details the practical process of what happens if someone would like to become my disciple and the Guru/ Disciple relationship in general. I also review the questions I had when I was a disciple.

33. A Bucket Full of Holes

A financial advisor tells me who is the biggest hole in our leaking bucket. I feel vulnerable regarding formal knowledge in terms of management, but let myself be guided by my understanding of human nature. The door of my office is always open.

34. Life in Our Hermitage

A day in the life at the Hermitage. I had built the ashram temple according to my Guru's instructions. It is now possible for me to stay in touch with my office, clients, and disciples via Internet.

35. Christian Fabre

After the demise of our Dude line, my staff chose my own birth-name, Christian Fabre, as our next brand name. I realise the purchasing power of domestic India. We target opening 150 stores all over India by 2012. In order to stay in touch with trends, I travel regularly with my design team to fashion fairs in Europe.

36. Sky-clad

The history and relevance of a naked swami in the 21st century is discussed. In India, I am called 'the naked emperor of the ready-to-wear industry'.

37. My Life and Friends in Chennai

I take the reader on a tour of daily life in the city at home and the office. Starting with my spiritual practice and then work. I introduce the important people close to me, Jayapalan, Pinky and Benhur.

38. Karma

Karma is the principle that governs my whole life and business ethic. Love is respect for one another and the ability to give without expecting anything in return, not only tolerance, but also acceptance.

39. In Meditation till the End of Time

I would love to be buried in our Hermitage in Kolli Hills, seated in the lotus position, so that I would be able to continue my meditation till the end of time.

To know more about Swamiji and his organisation contact:

bnpinky@gmail.com

swami.pranavananda@gmail.com

pinky@christianfabre.com

WEBSITES:

www.aumnamahshivaya.org.in

www.christianfabre.com

JAICO PUBLISHING HOUSE

Elevate Your Life. Transform Your World.

Established in 1946, Jaico Publishing House is the publisher of stellar authors such as Sri Sri Paramahansa Yogananda, Osho, Robin Sharma, Deepak Chopra, Stephen Hawking, Eknath Easwaran, Sarvapalli Radhakrishnan, Nirad Chaudhuri, Khushwant Singh, Mulk Raj Anand, John Maxwell, Ken Blanchard and Brian Tracy. Our list which has crossed a landmark 2000 titles, is amongst the most diverse in the country, with books in religion, spirituality, mind/body/spirit, self-help, business, cookery, humour, career, games, biographies, fiction, and science.

Jaico has expanded its horizons to become a leading publisher of educational and professional books in management and engineering. Our college-level textbooks and reference titles are used by students countrywide. The success of our academic and professional titles is largely due to the efforts of our Educational and Corporate Sales Divisions.

The late Mr. Jaman Shah established Jaico as a book distribution company. Sensing that independence was around the corner, he aptly named his company Jaico ("Jai" means victory in Hindi). In order to tap the significant demand for affordable books in a developing nation, Mr. Shah initiated Jaico's own publications. Jaico was India's first publisher of paperback books in the English language.

In addition to being a publisher and distributor of its own titles, Jaico is a major distributor of books of leading international publishers such as McGraw Hill, Pearson, Cengage Learning, John Wiley and Elsevier Science. With its headquarters in Mumbai, Jaico has other sales offices in Ahmedabad, Bangalore, Bhopal, Chennai, Delhi, Hyderabad and Kolkata. Our sales team of over 40 executives, direct mail order division, and website ensure that our books effectively reach all urban and rural parts of the country.

SINCE 1946